Put That Cell Phone Down and Look Me in The Eye

Bringing Civility and Respect Back to The Workplace at All Levels of Business

by

BRIAN C. HAGGERTY

BCH Enterprise, LLC
500 East Broward Blvd.
Suite 1710
Fort Lauderdale, FL 33394

ISBN-10:   061582014X
ISBN-13:   9780615820149

Dedicated to the students of Belleville High School
Belleville, NJ

"Macte animo! Generose puer sic itur ad astra"

Acknowledgements

There've been countless people in my life to whom I can credit the inspiration and evolution of my platform. While their names can fill a book itself, I would like to list the names of those who've encouraged, helped and supported the work that led to this book and the establishing of its message.

I would like to recognize my parents, Paul and Elaine Haggerty, who laid the foundation for a wonderful life with boundless opportunities and from whom I learned the invaluable lessons of character. To my dear friends, Michael Melham, Richard Yanuzzi and Tyler Feneck: thank you for encouraging and believing in what I've developed. To my cousin, Richie DiLascio; my friends, Rocco Mazza, Margaret Cenci-Frontera and Rob Esposito for your friendship, support, and for always being a great sounding-board. To my dear friend, Joe Longo, the members of the Belleville Board of Education; Helene Feldman, Russ Pagano, the administration and faculty whose opportunity they offered supported my bringing these skills and principles to the students of their district.

Thank you, Joan Taub and the Belleville Public Library and Information Center. And a very loving and big thank you to Orlando and Lorraine Saa for being the epitome of kindness, generosity, friendship and love.

Finally, to my incredible team: Carol Hoenig, Lori Ames, Austin Atwell, Ned MacPherson and Chris Maiorino—thank you for believing in and sharing my vision and making it possible!

Thank you all so very much for what will be the first of many in a series of books and learning products—as well as my dream for establishing a universal standard and framework for respect and civility for all of humanity. "Manus Multae, Cor Unum."

Introduction

"Put that cell phone down and look me in the eye!" How many times have you wanted to say that when you are trying to speak to someone—trying to tell them something you consider important—only to have them pay half-attention while their eyes dart between you and their mobile device? Today's young business upstarts, as well as successful CEOs, live in a world that is divided between a real human being and a technological device. There is no getting away from it. Today's young professionals entering into the workforce come from a generation that spends more time texting, tweeting, Instagramming, Facebooking, e-mailing, sharing, uploading and downloading than any other. While they are all quite adept at using emoticons and abbreviations in their mobile communication, they have lost the age-old art of personal, face-to-face, communication. While there is nothing wrong with technology and its use in today's modern world, making it in business today means that this generation must come to grips with knowing when they should and should not engage with the cyber world and when they should engage with real people.

But, keeping one's eyes affixed on his or her mobile device is not the only casualty in today's technological world of business. It spans far beyond knowing the difference between when to look at your mobile device and when to make eye contact and give attention to a real human being. It is the loss of social skills and how those skills allow for interpersonal relationships to build while establishing one's reputation—a reputation which means the difference between being successful in business and not, a reputation built upon a solid foundation of character. While it may be acceptable to have a conversation with friends and family through a text or tweet, what happens when you arrive for a job interview, are seeking advancement or promotion or have to attend a business meeting, a sales call or write an e-mail to a customer or client? Being successful in business today means knowing the difference between a virtual cyber world and what to do, how to dress, how to speak and how to act in the real world. Many businesses today do video-conferencing, which often saves money and time for travel that is no longer necessary; however, this does not mean that professionalism should be compromised in the process. And because so much of our lives are shared online for the world to see, what is the image that today's businessperson is portraying of him or herself? What written digital record is he or she leaving for all of eternity to read and form assumptions?

Despite all of our technology and its incredible conveniences, many of today's young business people are living a life out of social balance. They do not know how to reconcile the difference between their cyber/personal lives and their public and professional lives, and the effect each has upon their reputation and ultimate success in their chosen career. There is no line of delineation and no standards by which they shape and model their professional image and reputation. In essence, many of today's young professionals are becoming more and more socially awkward while the seasoned CEO is being told he or she must stay abreast when it comes to social media and, like most people, they, too, can be susceptible to its distracting charms. But is it really their fault? After all, while the young professionals may graduate with a degree in a specific area of study, are they taught what is personally expected of them in business? Is the CEO simply trying to stay competitive in a world where the Internet has changed many of the rules? Even so, that doesn't mean we should allow technology to call the shots.

Therefore, we must ask ourselves, what role models are held up by society that help younger people model their own behavior in accordance with traditional and accepted traits that will serve to make them stand out in business? Does wearing a "hoodie" to a sales call or a business meeting make someone appear successful because Mark Zuckerberg always wears one? Does showing up late for an appointment—even if only by three minutes—show someone how busy you are? When dining with a client, does placing your mobile device on the table within your view give the impression that you are connected and in demand? Does using slang or poor grammar not matter today in business because good grammar is almost never heard, much less recognized when it is?

Let's face it. Today's job market is more highly competitive than ever before. There are far more job candidates than there are jobs. If you have a job, keeping it is a challenge because efficiency and cost-saving could very well put your job on the chopping block. And what about advancement and promotion? Isn't that what everyone is seeking once they are working? How valuable do you really think you are? What kind of reputation have you established for yourself? Why should you—out of hundreds of other candidates—be given a job? Why should you—out of ten to thirty other candidates—be given a promotion? What makes you so different than the others? Is it the school from which you graduated? Is it the car you drive? How about your grade point average? The answer is it is none of those! No one particularly cares about what class you took in college, what your grades were or what fraternity you belonged to. In this highly competitive age where everyone is seeking to stand out from the rest, the words on a piece of paper describing how wonderful you are and what skills you posses may get you the interview, but not necessarily the position. The number of degrees hanging upon your wall won't really matter. Therefore, if you truly want to stand out from the rest and be successful in business today, you need to perfect your people skills. It is your people skills—the way you interact with others and how they perceive you—that will make you successful—ask any thriving businessman. If people like you, enjoy being in your company, trust you and can rely upon you, you will have a far greater advantage than someone who merely relies upon their written credentials.

So, maybe it's time to hang up the hoodie and keep it for the gym. Maybe it's time to put away your mobile device when you are speaking with someone and learn the art of conversation. Perhaps it's time to drop the slang and choose to be well spoken. And maybe, just maybe, it is time to refine and work on all of your character traits and personal skills, which will ultimately be the very skills that will make you a success! It's time to put away your childhood whimsies and get into the grown-up world where you will be assessed and judged by your people skills and character. Don't be like the masses. If you really want to stand out and get the position, the promotion or succeed in business, it's time to put that cell phone down, look people in the eye and show them who and what you are! It's your choice. It's your career. It's your life. Only you hold the power to stand out from the rest.

CHAPTER ONE

Successful Traits of Character

So you want to be a success? Who doesn't? But with the incredible amount of competition in today's business world, how exactly can you distinguish yourself to accomplish your goals, dreams and ambitions? How do you establish yourself as being valuable to a company, firm or client? What is it that makes a person appealing to others? What is it that will ultimately ensure your success in business?

It all boils down to your reputation. Your reputation is how you will be known to others. But reputation is all about your personal character and how your character applies to all that you do professionally.

I'd like for you to imagine that each of us has his or her own character rating. Think of this character rating as being similar to a credit rating. Good credit rating means being able to borrow more money at a lower interest rate. A good credit rating is the result of developing a "reputation" for being timely and responsible with your finances. While a good credit rating is important, people don't walk down the street with their credit score displayed on a sign around their neck. But, a good character rating becomes known for everyone by everyone around them. Just as a bank or credit company is far less apt to lend money to anyone whose credit rating is low, the people with whom we deal in business will also be less inclined to hire us, do business with us or promote us if your reputation is less than stellar.

Today's world of business is not only highly competitive; it is also fast-moving. Time is considered one of the most valuable of commodities. Deadlines, commitments, appointments, returning phone calls, e-mails and making meetings are all a part of our modern world of business. How you handle all of this, the manner in which you approach everything and your level of attention to detail and accomplishment is what will determine the way others assess you. And if you want that perfect job, desire that promotion or wish to acquire that client, this is the place to start!

The substance of your reputation can be described with one word: integrity. Integrity extends to every area of our professional lives. Its secret lies in being consistent, at all times, in your professional life and the extent to which it applies to the habits you display. A person with integrity is one who earns the trust and respect of those she or he works for or with. Yes! The greatest virtue you can possess in today's business world is integrity. Personal and professional integrity speak volumes to everyone else about who you are. Integrity begins with respect for yourself and respect for others. If you truly are serious about distinguishing yourself from others and demonstrating your worth to your company, clients or business associates, developing a reputation for integrity will do more for you than any degree or well-written resume can do and you will develop a powerful reputation that will cause you to excel in your business or profession. You will move ahead in your career far more quickly than others and will enjoy the respect and admiration of everyone.

In my own experiences in the world of business, I have had first-hand exposure to the irritating and annoying bad habits of many "professionals." Lateness for a meeting, the failure to complete something on time or see something through, the failure to follow up on something, the lack of, or lateness in, returning phone calls or e-mails in a timely manner are all the hallmarks of today's "average" business person. Sadly, these bad habits are far more common and rampant among today's business people than ever before. This is due, in part, to our becoming a more relaxed society where people spend more time on the Internet, send texts to friends all day long, post photos on Facebook, send tweets and engage in other activities that have taken the focus away from a work ethic and more toward self-stimulation. The good news is that if you make the conscious choice to establish a pristine reputation and reject all of the bad habits many professionals possess today, you are earning the greatest advantage over everyone else. These good habits of a professional have nothing to do with intelligence. They are not bestowed by a degree from a certain university. They can only become the traits of the person who makes the decision to fully integrate these traits into their lives and develop the habit of consistency by applying them to all that you do in your career.

Let's take a look at each of these traits and why they are important and lend to your advantage in today's business world by establishing your reputation among your professional peers.

1. Punctuality

*"I figured this was the easy stuff, and if we couldn't
show up on time, looking right and acting right, we
weren't going to be able to do anything else."*

—*Bo Schembechler, Bo's Lasting Lessons: The Legendary
Coach Teaches the Timeless Fundamentals of Leadership*

Among the rarest of traits of today's professional is punctuality.
If you make the decision to implement this trait you will be on
your way to becoming an outstanding professional. Do you show
up late for meetings? Even if only by a minute? Are you bad
with returning phone calls and e-mails in a timely manner? If
you have a project to complete, do you fail to complete it on
time or rush to complete it haphazardly? If you answered yes
to any of the above, then you are like most young professionals
today, a dime a dozen! But you don't want to be like the average
business professional. You want to be a success. You want to
stand out from the large array of modern-day business hopefuls
by holding yourself to a higher standard, a standard which only
you can set. Setting this standard begins with your recognizing
that in order to succeed in business, you need to no longer see
things as they apply to you. You must, instead, see things as they
apply to others and how, by doing so, you uphold and affirm
your reputation for being on time. You have to deflate your ego
and humble yourself. You absolutely need to understand that
the way you treat others in business and the manner in which
you hold their importance must always supersede your own
personal beliefs and desires.

A successful business person is always on time and always
returns phone calls and e-mails in a timely manner. When you do,

you are showing respect for the other person and their time and schedule. When you do this consistently, you develop a reputation as someone who is reliable; and reliability is one of the most valuable, yet rarest, of traits in the business world.

Think about it as if you are creating your own brand. The success of a product is the result of a quality, time-tested and trusted brand name. People will always spend more money on something if they know that it will work reliably. The same goes for an employer or a client. Do you think a company wants to waste its precious resources on someone who is not reliable? Do you believe that a client will do business with someone who fails to complete or deliver something on time? Of course not. That wouldn't even make sense. That's why it makes no sense to me that most younger business people today are so slipshod in their approach toward business. They've lulled themselves into a false reality-bubble where they are better and more adept at finding and creating an excuse for their failing to be somewhere, do something or complete something on time than they are at upholding their commitments. An excuse is about you and your failure to take personal responsibility to do what you need to do. A successful person makes no excuses. A successful person does whatever he or she needs to do in order to uphold their responsibility to their client or company. It's just that simple. There is no magic involved. Those who have a reputation for consistent punctuality and reliability will get ahead of those who do not. If something needs to get done, you get it done. You stay up all night; you don't go to the gym that night or stop at a bar to meet friends for a drink. You don't spend hours on Facebook or Twitter. You put everything in your personal life aside until you have completed what you said you would do.

Being Late for a Meeting Can Cost You More Than Time

The next time you think it is all right to show up a few minutes late for a meeting at the office, consider the Venture Capital Firm of Andreessen Horowitz who instituted a $10 fine for any of their employees who show up late for meetings. $10 per minute, that is! The firm's co-founder, Ben Horowitz explained, "When you're an entrepreneur, you work around the clock, you visit venture capital firms and the very first thing that you get is you sit in the lobby for 45 minutes waiting for them." Horowitz explained that it is not about the money so much as it is to emphasize the importance of not keeping entrepreneurs waiting in the lobby.

The Moral of the Story: *Time is money and everyone's time is valuable.*

Source: MediaBistro.com
"Employer Fines Workers $10 Each Minute For Being Tardy to Meetings"

Today's young business person often talks about how tired they are or how stressed out they may be. Yet, they find time to post on Facebook, Twitter and even play games on Wii or PlayStation. "I need my down time," they say. But if you were to add up all of the time they spend each day on social media, they could have completed all of their responsibilities for the day without excuse. And, if you are one whose day is spent uploading photos or posting your opinions about last night's episode of *Survivor* or *American Idol* on Facebook, don't think your boss, manager or client isn't watching. If you don't uphold your commitments and wind up making excuses while you are spending valuable time on social media, you are basically sending the message that your client or company is not as important as your social media life. If this is the case, you've already lost that promotion. In fact, the effect of our social media lives has an even greater reach in our professional lives that goes beyond wasting our time. It's an extension of who we are and an advertisement to the world about our personal "brand." I will explain this extension in greater detail in a subsequent chapter, but for now you need to understand that unless you set your professional priorities where your responsibilities are at the top you will not be among those who succeed in business.

2. Reliability

"A man who lacks reliability is utterly useless."

—Confucius (551-479)

People will always find the time for the things they like to do. Few make time for the things they need to do. In business, if you want to succeed, you must be among those who will always make time for the things that you need to do. Don't expect that you will get that promotion or secure that client if they feel that they are second to your own personal whimsies. If you want to be a winner in business, then you must have a reputation for reliability. There is an old expression in business, which says, "If you want something done, give it to the busy person." Busy people always seem to have the time to get things done. Yet, all I hear today among most of the younger business people is that they have no time for anything. But, a closer look at the average business upstart shows a different reality. It is not that they don't have the time. It's that they don't want to make the time to do the things they need to do to truly succeed. They find the time to spend on social media, watch YouTube clips, talk endlessly on their cell phone, send texts back and forth to their friends all day, go to the gym, watch their favorite television shows and spend several hours engaged in their respective hobbies. If this is how you choose to spend your time, then don't expect to succeed in business.

No one ever said that it is fun or pleasurable to spend long hours at the office to finish a report, or drive hours to meet a client. Giving up sleep to finalize your project or meet a deadline never rates up high on our list of things we like to do. But if we want to be successful, truly successful, then the desire to be successful should supersede all of our other desires. If it does not, then you can count on a career where you find yourself in an aimless drift with no goals, no achievement and nothing but a list of excuses to make you feel better about yourself and your lack of success. There is no one else to blame except yourself.

If you develop your personal brand of reliability, you'll never have a shortage of opportunity to advance yourself. You will never have to worry that someone else may pass you over. Reliability is another of the rarest of professional traits whose value cannot be understated. It means that you have been tested and can be trusted.

3.   Humility

"Do you wish to rise? Begin by descending. You plan
a tower that will pierce the clouds? Lay first the
foundation of humility."

—*St. Augustine (354-430)*

No character trait is more powerful than humility. And no one is more detested than one who thinks extremely highly of him or herself. No one likes a person with a large ego. Arrogance should never be mistaken for confidence and will certainly not gain you any favor in the world of business. Humility speaks more loudly than any boast. In fact, most big egos are the result of insecurity. No one likes a boss or a manager who is arrogant. No one will want to work with someone who is ego-driven. Humility shows others that you are a team player. People will always be far more likely to assist you, help you and share with you when you are humble.

All of your abilities, every talent, your intellect and your accomplishments will speak for themselves. A person of humility never seeks approval. Never brag or talk about how good you are at something. When you are humble and never seek the acknowledgment of your accomplishments, there are no worries, for others will do that for you. And the person of humility will always seek to compliment, praise and acknowledge the achievements, deeds and abilities of others. If only everyone truly understood that the secret to being noticed and acknowledged by others comes only from humility, imagine how wonderful and fulfilling every workplace would be. Let me conclude the topic of humility with a quote attributed to Socrates: "I know that I am intelligent, because I know that I know nothing."

4.   Kindness

"Carry out a random act of kindness, with no expectation of reward, safe in the knowledge that one day someone might do the same for you."

—*Princess Diana*

Kindness is contagious. Everyone wants to be treated with kindness. It brings out the best in people and is warming to the soul. If you want to achieve in your career, always show kindness to everyone, everywhere at every opportunity. Demonstrating kindness in business does not make you appear weak. It will not make you vulnerable. It is part of your overall character. People would rather work with and do business with someone whom they know to be kind. Managers want this type of atmosphere in their workplace. Employees work harder and have a far greater work ethic when they are treated kindly. Customers will always return when treated kindly. Clients, business associates and contacts will always look forward to doing business when the atmosphere is one of kindness.

Consider this: hard-nosed, gruff business people are becoming a thing of the past. After all, with all of today's competition in the workplace, the more choices people have for their working conditions and their business associates, the more apt they will be to choose to deal with people who are kind.

5. Respect

"I firmly believe that respect is a lot more important, and a lot greater, than popularity."

—*Julius Irving*

You cannot expect to achieve great heights in your career unless you are respected by others. Respect, however, is not automatic. It must be earned. The only way to earn respect is to demonstrate it to everyone—at all times. You cannot earn respect from others with the car you drive or the school from which you graduated. It cannot come from your looks or from your name. It can only come from the manner in which you treat and speak to others. As you continue to layer each of the traits of character in this chapter upon one another, and make them a part of your nature, respect is the one which will cement your reputation among others and afford you the power that comes from its juices.

People want to be respected. They want their opinions, religion, ethnicity and humanity to be respected by all. But respect is a two-way street. It is a back and forth motion with an expression that yields its own fruit. When you demonstrate respect to others, they will demonstrate it to you. It is that simple. Respect involves each of the traits we have discussed so far. But it mostly involves humility. It involves putting others ahead of you, deferring to others and valuing them as human beings who, just like you, are in pursuit of their dreams. Success in your career depends upon how people perceive you and whether or not they like you. Where you may lack in ability, intellect or knowledge in your job or career, being respectful can and will fill those voids in the eyes of others in a way nothing can. How can anyone not like someone who is respectful? Who can find fault in one who finds no fault in others? Once you are regarded as a most respectful professional, others will overlook many of your flaws.

In business, people want to work with and do business with those who make them feel comfortable. A professional in business may have intellect and abilities that are superior. But unless you are viewed favorably, unless you make your peers, customers, clients and co-workers feel comfortable, you will not even have the opportunity to demonstrate such superior ability because no one will want to be around you, much less work with you or for you. In other words, you will need to earn respect. Let's take a look at some examples of respect and how it affects those around us.

Respect begins with your making the conscious decision to put others before you. You want to start with the intention of making everyone feel comfortable, welcomed and important. Let's say you walk into your office building in the morning at the start of the work day. Is there a doorman or person working at the counter who checks people into the building? If so, make sure to say "good morning" to that person with a smile on your face. Ask them, "How are you today?" But be sure to listen to their answer. Demonstrating interest in others is not only respectful, but it shows sophistication. It will usually be appreciated. Each person is a unique human being and has his or her own lives, family, dreams and desires. A warm greeting, a smile and interest in their well-being will show them that you are a kind, gracious and caring human being. Get to know their name and make sure you address them with it each time you see them. Learn about their family, their children and their hobbies. Show them that you care. You have no idea how powerful this is and how people will respond to you as a result. By showing them your respect as a human being, you are earning theirs.

When you walk into your office, don't wear your problems on your face. Everyone has his or her own problems in life with which they deal on a daily basis. So, never think you are alone in your problems. Instead, do everything you can to think about the things in your life that make you happy. Put your cares away and recognize that a smile and a friendly hello to someone else will spark happiness within them. Is there a receptionist when you walk into your office? If so, extend a warm and happy good morning and ask them how they are that day. The more you are seen as a person who is kind and considerate, the more people will become attracted to you. Everyone will love to be around you and be happy to see you.

Keep mental notes on the important things in other people's lives. Is today their birthday? Be sure to wish them a very happy birthday. Is a family member ill? Make sure you ask them about that person. Is their son or daughter awaiting acceptance into a college? Ask them how that's going. Did something nice happen in their lives such as the birth of a child, a new car or an achievement? Recognize that great event in their life and take delight in their joy.

Did someone do something nice for you? Did they perhaps give you a birthday gift or help you with a project? If so, send them a handwritten thank you note and thank them for their kindness and thoughtfulness. This will leave a lasting impression upon them while showing them that you are a sophisticated and thoughtful person. A handwritten note is very special. I've kept every single note anyone has ever sent to me and chances are they will keep yours.

Does someone need a hand carrying something? Help them to carry it. When you walk through a swinging door, always look behind you to see if someone else is there. Smile and hold the door until they arrive to grab it from you. Are they carrying something in their arms? Hold the door open for them and allow them to enter. Maybe it is a mother pushing a baby carriage or an elderly person. Or maybe it is an employee trying to manage a briefcase, box of files and handbag. Again, hold the door for them and allow them to pass while offering assistance. Greet everyone with a smile and a warm hello. And if such kindness doesn't evoke a response from someone, don't be sarcastic. We never know where someone's thoughts lie or what's going on in their lives. Always be the better person. We don't show respect only to those who show it to us. We show respect to everyone because that is the kind of person we need to be. If two people are speaking and you need to walk by between them, always say "excuse me" before doing so.

Respect is all about making others feel better about themselves. A successful person is one who seeks to lift others up while treating them with complete dignity. Remember, to be a truly successful professional in your career, you will only achieve that success when you treat others with respect, hold them in high esteem and acknowledge the successes in their own lives. What you extend to others will be returned to you.

6. **Truthfulness**

"I found that the more truthful and vulnerable I was,
the more empowering it was for me."

—Alanis Morissette

The concept of being truthful involves a great deal more than a mere telling of the truth. Everyone knows it is wrong to lie and no one likes a liar. But the trait of truthfulness extends to a full acceptance of our strengths and weaknesses, as well as our candor in admitting what we can and cannot do.

The successful professional must embody truthfulness. People generally fear rejection. As a result, people create a false identity and hide behind a cloak of deceit to protect their fragile self- esteem. The problem is that most people—especially in business—fear being wrong. They worry that any mistake they make may harm them in their advancement. This is the false reality under which most professionals live. They may say, "If my manager finds out I made this mistake, she'll be really mad!" And so, they begin the age old art of the cover-up. They try to cover their tracks, deny knowledge of something or attempt to cause distraction away from them and on to another co-worker or another thing. Sir Walter Scott's famous quote, "Oh, what a tangled web we weave when first we practice to deceive", tells of a deeper truth which involves all deception. It is not easy to tell a lie. Not only do you need to make sure that everything surrounding your lie matches the other parts of your story, but you also must remember everything you said in your lie. It is very difficult to keep up a lie. And the truth about lying is that eventually a lie is revealed. The more you lie, the more lying you have to do to keep up with the original one.

The truth, on the other hand, is always easy. It never changes, is easy to remember and will always stand up to scrutiny. Truth is liberating! If you worry that someone will think less of you because you made a mistake, you are living under a delusion. You are allowing your ego to stand in the way of an opportunity to actually increase your personal power and reputation. When you admit a fault or a mistake, you are demonstrating your humanity and humility. No one will dislike you for merely telling the truth. Telling the truth means being accepting of all of your weaknesses and shortcomings. After all, each has his or her own strengths and weaknesses. Some are better at certain things than others. So what? After all, any good manager will tell you that they want to know each person's abilities and inabilities in their office or company in order to fully integrate and make use of each person's talents and abilities.

Telling the truth is a sign of self-respect and respect for others. It respects their time, their intelligence and builds rapport and strength in any group. If you aim to please everyone to the point that you will never admit your faults, weaknesses or mistakes, you are only digging a hole for yourself in which you will eventually fall. Once people cannot trust you or your word, you lose all credibility. No one will want to do business with you and you will not move ahead in your career.

Telling the truth shows that you are a secure person who takes responsibility for everything you do. If you tell your boss that you can do something, but know that you are not truly able to do it, yet fear your boss thinking that you are not worth as much as you would like her to think, understand that she will ultimately find out that you cannot do the required task. When that happens, do you think her opinion of you will increase or decrease? When opportunities for promotion come up, do you think she will recommend you? On the other hand, what if your boss comes and asks you to do something and you, being truthful, admit with candor that you do not feel you are able to do it? First of all, you are showing respect to your boss by not wasting her time on thinking you can accomplish something. But, you are also earning the respect of your boss who will greatly appreciate your candor and not forget it. Now let's take this even further. If your boss does ask you to do something and you feel you are not able to accomplish the given task, your honesty will go a long way. She will probably ask you why you feel you are not capable of doing the task and will most likely then assist you in any way you need by either pointing you in the right direction or assigning someone else to assist you in the areas in which you feel you lack adequate experience or knowledge. Because you were truthful, you earned the respect of your boss and—as a result—were given the resources and assets with which to actually perform the task, and you wound up learning how to do something completely new.

Think about how refreshing it is when you are told the truth by someone. Suppose you are relying upon someone else telling you they can do something for you only to find out that they can't? How does that make you feel? On the other hand, if someone admits to you that they are unable to do something or accomplish something, do you hate them for it? Do you hold them in contempt? Of course you don't. You appreciate it. You feel refreshed and you wind up trusting that person and respecting them. The same goes for you in your dealings in business. Let your yes be yes and your no be no. Admit your faults, weaknesses and handicaps. No one will recoil away from you. In fact, they will become more attracted to you, trusting of you, and in business this will make you soar on the highway toward your desired dreams of success!

CONCLUDING REMARKS

The character you display in all that you do will shape your reputation. When you are consistent in your character, you will develop the trust of those around you. You will earn the respect that will allow for you to advance in your job and career. Most employers surveyed rate soft skills far higher than technical knowledge. Therefore, strong, solid character is vital in your relationships and in how you deal with others. If you learn one thing in this first chapter, please let it be that your ultimate success in business will be determined by how you relate to others.

While technical knowledge is certainly important, human beings respond to the elements of character that define a person as kind, humble, gracious and respectful. No matter your level of intelligence or expertise, without the elements of character as your foundation, others will not wish to do business with you or work with you. Good character trumps technical skills. Therefore, when going for a job interview, seeking a promotion or attempting to acquire a new client, the manner in which you display your character will do more for you to achieve than having a genius I.Q.

CHAPTER TWO

Presence & Presentation

"Few delights can equal the presence of one whom we trust utterly."

—George MacDonald, Scottish novelist, clergyman and author of children's stories

If you have fully understood and absorbed the greatest and most powerful traits of character in Chapter One, you have laid a solid foundation for your success in your business or career. With such a strong foundation, you can now begin to build upon it and add to the totality of your overall persona that will increase your confidence and contribute to your success. A person of strong character already has the advantage over him or her who does not. But a person of strong character who also develops a great presence and presentation has an even greater advantage.

The process of developing a strong presence begins with self-awareness. If you are of strong character, people will already be endeared and attracted to you. But, in order to gain that edge in business, have that truly successful interview, acquire that account or client, or make the top of the list for promotions, establishing a strong presence is your second stop in your journey of becoming the best you can be. With six billion people in the world, you wonder how someone can stand out. Well, you don't need to engage in theatrics or drama to get attention. You most certainly don't need to or should not talk about yourself. Let your presence speak for itself. Developing your presence involves several factors. One, you must become self-aware, aware of how you walk, stand, dress and gesture. Second, you need to understand timing and how it relates to human interaction and relationships. Third, you need to make the conscious choice to practice and implement these things into the fiber of your being. Presence has a great deal to do with how you see and perceive yourself. It begins from within by holding mental images of yourself that project the kind of person you are—and believe yourself to be—to the outside world.

Let's start our discussion about presence by taking a look at celebrities. Most celebrities have presence. They have cultivated and developed it for many years and it shows. You can have the same presence in business as a celebrity does on the red carpet purely by making the conscious decision to become aware of a few key things and taking the steps to change and correct various things about yourself.

HOW DO YOU SEE YOURSELF?

Our state of mind and the self-image we hold of ourselves may be internal, but this inner belief about ourselves will affect the way we appear outwardly. If you are a shy person who lacks confidence, this belief about yourself will affect your posture, your walk and the expression on your face. Success in business has a great deal to do with image. If we exude an image of confidence and happiness, this image will shine through for others to see. Confidence, as opposed to arrogance, is a very seductive and attractive quality in people. Most people unfortunately lack confidence. Confidence is merely a belief in yourself. It has nothing to do with thinking you are better than others; that is arrogance. Confidence, on the other hand, means you know who you are and are comfortable in your own skin and are aware of your strengths, weaknesses, talents, abilities and inabilities. It doesn't mean you believe yourself to be perfect. A truly confident person recognizes what he or she is capable of accomplishing while being completely accepting and at ease with his or her flaws. Confidence is inspiring! Contagious! It is motivating! A confident person heaps praise on others for their accomplishments and abilities. A confident person does not fear that someone else is trying to supersede their efforts at work or sabotage them for the next advancement or promotion. Instead, a confident person has a quiet peace that allows everyone in their presence to feel at ease and be the best that they can be.

If you want to be successful in business, then you need to feel successful. You must believe that you are a success. You have to develop confident thoughts that will build your self-image and allow for you to project the image of success. This belief in yourself will surely grow as you continue to visualize yourself the way you want others to perceive you.

SMILE

All people seek the same thing—happiness. We love to be around happy people because they make us feel happy. Therefore, when we see someone smile, we are automatically attracted to them because a smile is contagious and represents happiness. If we want to develop our presence and make a lasting, wonderful impression on everyone we meet in business, then smiling is the way to start.

According to a survey conducted by Kelton Global, first positive impressions all come down to the power of an attractive smile. So if you are headed to a job interview, a meeting, a networking event or are having a headshot taken for your LinkedIn profile, make sure

---

Smile Your Way Toward Success!

According to a survey conducted by Kelton Global on behalf of the American Academy of Cosmetic Dentistry, first positive impressions all come down to the power of an attractive smile. The survey showed that 48 percent of adults think a smile is the most memorable feature after they meet someone for the first time. This is even more powerful than the spoken word which raked in 25 percent of respondents. The way someone dresses pulled in nine percent and the way someone smells got eight percent of respondents. If you have crooked or stained teeth, this survey proves the value in investing in a good dentist and some teeth whitener! Next time you go to a job interview, a networking meeting or meet a client for the first time, remember to flash those pearly whites!

Moral of the Story: Smile and the world smiles back!

Source: MediaBistro.com Author: Vicki Salemi
Article: "New Survey Shows Smiling is the Best Way to Make a First Impression"
February 26, 2013
*Survey: American Academy of Cosmetic Dentistry

---

you flash those pearly whites. In fact, just the mere act of smiling has a positive effect on the way you feel. Smiling actually releases endorphins into your blood stream, which act as natural pain killers. In fact, our whole physiology changes when we smile. It lowers our blood pressure, boosts our immune system and actually makes us look younger. There is every reason to smile; not only for success, but also because it is a natural way to help us to feel better.

Work on your smile. It is possible that some people may need dental work to correct or straighten their teeth. Or, perhaps your teeth are stained from tobacco, coffee or red wine. Either way, try to whiten those teeth and perhaps invest in some invisible braces, if need be. It will be well worth it. A smile is one of the most powerful instruments in our personal presence and presentation. It's the first thing people will notice about you.

Admittedly, some people do not smile. Others don't feel like smiling. Even more do not feel they have a nice smile. It is important that you don't try to "put on" a smile. A fake smile is as noticeable as a bad toupee, but a real smile always reveals itself. If you are one who does not smile, or does not like your smile, the way to have a natural and real smile is to think of things that make you happy. In fact, you should develop the habit of always thinking about the things that make you happy. It could be thinking about doing the things you love. It could be about your children, your friends or a time in your life when you were most happy about something. Either way, holding the mental image in your mind of those things that make you happy will make it very easy for you to display a natural, real and endearing smile. Make the conscious decision to become a person who smiles. Look at yourself in the mirror when you practice. Maybe too big of a smile does not work for you. Find the smile that works best and looks the greatest. It changes your entire countenance and exudes wondrous warmth that will draw people toward you and make them smile, too.

POSTURE

In addition to your smile, your posture is the next thing to work on. Good posture, like a smile, denotes confidence. When you walk into a job interview, a meeting or a networking event, your posture also sends a message about your level of confidence—while adding to your presence. If you walk with your head down or your shoulders slouched, you will not look confident. You won't have that presence which says you are ready to take on the world. Instead, you want to convey to others that you are vibrant, alert and ready to work. Having good posture is merely about standing with your chin level with the floor. If you are not sure how your posture looks, try to take a video of yourself standing and walking. The camera never lies. You will notice a great number of things about the way you look just by watching yourself on video. Try to develop the habit of keeping your chin level and looking outward. Get into the habit of using your eyes, rather than your head, to look down while you are walking. You want people to see your face. You want them to see your smile, your eyes, and to feel the confidence and happiness exuding directly from you.

Like every skill mentioned in this book, you must make the conscious decision to improve upon each one. Good posture is absolutely something you can gain merely by working at it. In the beginning, you will have to keep reminding yourself to stand and walk with that confident, impressive stride. But as time goes by, your good posture will become a habit—like every skill you develop. You will no longer have to think about your posture because you will have implemented it into the fabric of your being. Remember, all of our outward appearance is the result of what we are feeling and thinking inwardly. Make sure you keep visualizing in your mind the level of confidence, happiness and success that you want to convey. See yourself as successful. Feel your success. Surround yourself with successful people. In a short period of time, as you have practiced these skills, you will find yourself exuding all of the traits you have visualized inside of yourself while no longer having to consciously think about them. They will have become a habit; a good habit, a habit of success.

DRESS

Have you ever looked at old pictures, television shows or movies and noticed that everyone always seemed to look their best? Everyone's hair was neat and their clothes were clean and pressed. Men wore hats, women gloves and children stood quietly by their parents' side. People carried themselves in a manner that seemed dignified and upheld a sense of confidence in who they were. There was little chance for self-expression and few choices in one's wardrobe, but yet all seemed like they were ready to walk down the red carpet of celebridom. When anyone left their home, they were put together. Maybe they didn't have designer clothing and perhaps they wore little jewelry, but when it came to their personal presentation, they seemed to have a certain something that gave them presence.

Today, there are countless fashions of wardrobe, endless styles of hair, seemingly limitless color combinations and manners of dress; all of this is in the name of individuality. After all, people want to express themselves and be noticed. How else can one stand out in a world of six billion people and counting? People have more clothing, shoes, jewelry and accessories than any generation before. They are a walking billboard advertising their own individuality and personality—and also a designer's brand name. You may see a couple walking hand-in-hand, each with a shirt that says, "I'm with stupid." It's common to see a teenager with an explicit message scrawled across his back that indicates his disdain for society. Fashion has made it possible to advertise to the world where one fits in. Techies, bikers, athletes, drop-outs, metal-heads, trendies, new-agers, rappers, skaters, gamers, hunters, moshers, goths, punks, emo, liberals, conservatives and just about any self-identified group has a style of dress associated with who they are. A walk down a city street will yield more self-expression than can be counted. Yet, despite the public's fervent attempt to stand-out and be noticed, these countless groups seem to meld into one another and fade from our view. The individuality they seek is lost in a sea of societal static and white noise. Their walking billboards of self-expression have failed and they are without the very thing that makes people notice others—presence!

Have you heard the old expression "clothes don't make the person, the person makes the person"? Herein is the key to the secret of individuality and self-expression. Today's young upstarts venture out into the world of business with their sights set upon the fulfillment of their fervent dreams. But lost within this sea of self-expression is the age-old art of dressing professionally. Knowing how to dress appropriately in business is all a part of our personal presentation, which adds to our presence. It comes from inside of us. Its power is greater than any label; its attraction is more ravishing than any garment, and its effect is more potent than any color combination. It rejects any and all ideas imposed upon it from others. It holds within it the key to attraction and personal magnetism.

If you want to succeed in business and be credible in a business setting, then learn how to dress professionally. A hoodie, a backward baseball cap, sagging jeans and multiple body piercings are a guarantee that you won't be taken seriously. In fact, you may very well scare most people away. But beyond this, the way we dress and carry ourselves is what makes an immediate impression upon others. When you walk into an interview or arrive at a meeting, you want to signal that you are there to do business. You want others to see your attention to detail by the professional way you dress.

Perception is reality. If you look like a professional, others will believe you are. Unfortunately, today's younger generation does not take dressing all too seriously. After all, Mark Zuckerberg became a billionaire wearing a hoodie, flip flops and jeans. But you are not Mark Zuckerberg. He is the exception, not the rule. While his success in changing the world of social media is apparent, modeling yourself after him probably will not work unless you have a multibillion dollar concept that will also change the world.

For the rest of us in business, being well dressed, clean and neat is the way to go. Whenever we step out into the public eye, we should dress, act and walk as if there is a camera upon us at all times. What impression do you want others to have of you? Do you want others to take note of you in a good way or a bad way? Do you want people to treat you like the important person you want to be? Because people's clothes are so symbolic today of their personality, it's important to understand the message our clothes send to others; dressing well means paying attention to the details. And if you pay attention to the details of your dress, then that sends the message that you pay attention to the details of your business. It is a subconscious way of communicating to others what we're all about. In addition, if we pay no heed to our clothes, then that says we don't pay attention to things outside of us. This is why dressing well is more about others. If you want to kick around the house in sweatpants and tee-shirts, that's fine. Most do. But the moment you walk outside and are ready for business, picture that imaginary camera waiting to catch a glimpse of you. See yourself as you would appear in the eyes of the public. Well-dressed people are treated with respect. It's just that simple. They appear successful. And, the manner of your dress will wind up affecting how you perceive yourself and ultimately will affect the way you act.

Do your clothes make you look successful?

According to a series of studies published in the Evolution and Human *Behavior journal last year, flashing designer brands can provide an advantage. When wearing perceived high-status clothing, people gained cooperation from others more easily, scored job recommendations and higher salary, and received higher contributions for charity.*

- *Man wearing a polo shirt featuring a designer logo was rated as higher status as same man with logo photoshopped out.*

- *A female wearing a sweater with a designer logo got response rate of 52% (versus 13% of female wearing sweater sans logo) when asking passersby to fill out a survey.*

- *Participants watching a man interviewing for job on video rated the one with a shirt with a designer logo as more suitable for the job and deserving of a 9% higher salary than the same man without a logo.*

- *Wearing a designer logo resulted in twice as many contributions when soliciting for charity.*

Moral of the Story: *Wear the clothes that match the income you want to earn!*

Source: intuit.com Article Author: Eva Rykrsmith
Study: Social benefits of luxury brands as costly signals of wealth and status.
Authors: Rob M.A. Nelissen and Marijn H.C. Meijers

MAKING AN ENTRANCE

Now that you have learned the importance of having a presence that communicates to others that you are confident, happy, approachable, professional and friendly, it's time to put all of your presence to work every time you make an entrance.

Shakespeare said in his play, *As You Like It*, "All the world's a stage; And all the men and women merely players. They have their entrances and exits." When we are out and about in public—whether we are walking on the street, at the store or arriving at some sort of function or business meeting, we are on the stage of life. We are in public. This is when we can completely control how we look, dress and carry ourselves. This is our chance to show people who we are. If we want to be successful, then we want to be sure we are sending signals that tell people that we are someone with whom they would like to do business or hire. After all, we all like nice people, don't we? Well, that also translates to the business world. So the very first thing we want to do is send the signal that we are nice and that we are approachable.

You may not even realize it, but each time we walk into a room filled with people, we always get their attention. This is where you can learn how to take advantage of a universal human quirk that we all have and can be used to your advantage once you become consciously aware of it. Have you ever noticed that when you are in a room with a group of people and someone either gets up from their seat or walks into the room, everyone all of a sudden takes a quick look at that person? It's true. Yourself included. Everyone always takes a very quick look at whoever it is walking into the room or getting up from his or her seat. It is a natural human distraction. And it does not matter if someone important is speaking in the front of the room. The moment someone stands up or walks in, the entire room of people turns its attention for one split second toward that person. Well, guess what, you can learn how to take advantage of that human quirk and use it to burn an image into everyone's mind as to the kind of person you are. You have that one split second to make a first impression. In that one split second, you can send a multitude of non-verbal cues to everyone else in the room. The key is to send the right cues. You never know who is going to be in a meeting, at a networking event or chamber of commerce luncheon. That's why you always want to look professional, confident, happy and approachable. Each is among the greatest qualities that will help you succeed in your career.

MAKING THE ENTRANCE

There is a right way to make an entrance and a wrong way. Most make an entrance the wrong way because they are not aware of the power of the entrance. In fact, most are not even aware of the non-verbal body language they are unwittingly sending forth. Making a good entrance does not involve a dramatic display of movement. It involves good posture, a smile, good eye contact and timing. But before we discuss how to make a good entrance, we should discuss the wrong way to make an entrance because that is the kind of entrance a majority of people make.

HOW NOT TO MAKE AN ENTRANCE

We now know that achieving success involves good people skills and strong character. But unfortunately, most people are shy. They are shy because they do not have the self-confidence to meet new people. They do not know how to introduce themselves, much less have a conversation. Too many people send out the wrong non-verbal cues because they are subconsciously trying to avoid meeting people. But a successful business professional not only wants to meet new people, he or she *needs* to meet new people.

Today, it has never been easier to avoid encountering people. If you are shy and don't like meeting people, you have at your disposal the greatest and worst invention of all time—the Smartphone or a similar mobile device. Thanks to these handheld mobile communication devices, you can now bury your face into its screen. While you may think you are showing everyone how busy you are, you are actually precluding yourself from making the connections you will need to be successful. And, this is exactly what most people today are doing. When most people walk into a room, a meeting, a restaurant, a party, etc., they are looking down at their mobile device, not out at the room filled with people. As a result, when everyone else in the room takes that quick, split-second glance at them as they walk into the room, all they see is the top of the person's head. They do not see their eyes, they do not see someone who looks interesting and they do not see someone who is interested in meeting them. All they see is someone who is ordinary; someone who is doing what everyone else today seems to be doing. The opportunity to grab people's attention for that split second and make a host of non-verbal impressions is lost. But, the reality is that most people do not want to make an impression. They would rather hide behind their mobile device and keep their focus on the screen.

If you want to be a success and wish to develop your people skills for business, then the first thing you need to do is put your mobile device away! Whenever you are with real human beings, your mobile device should never be out, but should be in your pocket. Have you ever been with a friend, trying to tell them a story and, as you are telling your story, they are nodding at you while checking or reading something on their mobile device? How does that make you feel? If you are like everyone else, it makes you feel disrespected because the message being sent to you is that the person or message on the mobile device is of more importance than you. Now the question becomes have you ever checked or been reading messages on your mobile device when someone is speaking to you? The answer is most likely yes. In business, we must give one hundred percent of our attention to the person with whom we are speaking. Any time we whip out our mobile device in the presence of a customer, client, business associate, manager or co-worker, we are showing them disrespect and sending the message that they are of less importance than what is on your mobile device.

Don't misunderstand; mobile phones are a great invention. But they have completely taken over our lives and have become a crutch for people who lack personal skills. They have hampered a generation from learning how to interact and communicate with real human beings. They have made it too easy to remove yourself from a room by putting your face into its screen. And when you do so, you do not have to fear speaking to anyone. The problem with this is that if you truly want to be successful, you need to know how to meet people. You should be anxious to meet people. Once you know the mechanics of it, it is easy and you will look forward to doing so at every occasion. So, the first thing you need to learn, if you want to make an entrance and get to know people, is to put your mobile device away! If you are in the habit of checking it every few minutes, break that habit. Turn it off, if you have to. It is the biggest distraction there is to meeting and speaking to people face to face. Put it away and get ready to make an entrance the proper way.

HOW TO MAKE AN ENTRANCE

Now that you have put your phone away, I want you to mentally picture yourself walking into a room filled with people. Remember, when you walk into the room, everyone within eye view is going to take a very quick look at you—albeit unconsciously. It is this human quirk of which you will take advantage. In fact, when done correctly, you will turn what is otherwise a split-second glance and turn it into a notice that lasts an extra split-second. You are going to do this because you are going to make an impression upon everyone in the room—a good impression!

The first thing you will do before you walk into a room is to make sure your posture is good. Remember, good posture denotes confidence and well-being. The easiest way to keep your posture is to keep your chin level with the floor. Do not be looking up or down. Make sure you are looking outward. Make sure you observe everyone in the room taking notice of you.

As you approach the doorway into the room, become aware of how you look. Keep your gaze looking outward and think of anything that makes you happy. This is the prime opportunity to make sure, as well, that you are donning that smile of yours. Remember to visualize something that makes you happy so your smile is real. With your posture in place and wearing a smile, you are prepared to walk into the room.

As you walk through the doorway, you should have the intention of making eye contact with as many people in the room as you can and remember to look at everyone. Step to the right or left—out of the way of others—and pause for a moment. Take in the room and everyone who is in it. You should look happy, approachable and open to meeting everyone. Make sure your attention is on the room and everyone in it. You will notice that people are looking back at you—even if they are in conversation with others. You will notice some are smiling back at you—even if they do not realize it. What you are doing is sending forth all sorts of non-verbal cues as to the kind of person you are. You are real, safe, confident and happy. Because you are there to meet people, you are sending that message and people will absolutely want to meet you. The people in the room will actually take a longer note of you. You are burning an image into their subconscious mind that will stay with them. Now, as you work your way throughout the room all evening, people will actually remember you from your entrance. Perhaps they won't know you or your name, but they will already know that they like you and will be very interested in meeting you. This is because you will represent the very things most people are seeking: happiness and confidence.

This is an amazing skill to experience in action. And once you do it, you will realize just how powerful it is. Not only will you get over your shyness, but you will have more conversations than ever before because you will meet more people. In fact, they will want to meet you. Always remember that if the majority of our success in life comes from our people skills, then we need to develop those skills by meeting as many people as possible. It's called networking. The more people we meet, the more connections we make, the more doors open for us in business. It is how successes are written.

Knowing how to introduce yourself, shake hands and how to introduce others is also an art form that you can learn and practice. But before we explore that, let's discuss how to walk and the way it adds to our presence.

HOW YOU WALK

In addition to the way we dress, the way we walk also expresses a great deal about our level of awareness and self-confidence. Like all of our presentation and presence, we can consciously change the way we walk. Assuming you do not have a physical disability, which affects your walk, start to take note of your walk. How does your gait appear? Are you walking with your head up? Do you have a confident stride? Or, does your walk make you appear shy, reserved and unfriendly?

Look at celebrities and national politicians. If you think they are not aware of their walk and have not taken steps throughout their career to change and improve it, you are mistaken. Celebrities and politicians are among the most self-aware people in society. They have studied and changed their appearance throughout their lives to always express confidence—even if they are being slandered in the papers.

When models go to modeling school, they are taught how to walk. They work on their posture and their gait. They understand that the way they walk is an integral part of how they will be perceived. In fact, just dressing up will affect the way you walk. You will feel better about yourself. Therefore, it all begins with how we see ourselves and the way we perceive ourselves inwardly. Successfully-minded people are filled with thoughts and ideas about success. They fill their mind with images of themselves being successful. You will become more and more aware of the way you look and how others perceive you.

If you want to be noticed when you walk into a room, a meeting, a board room or just down the street, the first thing you need to do is get your eyes off of your mobile device and look out at the world. Just keep your eyes looking outward will make you walk straight. Keep those shoulders squared off. Swing your arms back and forth and always be thinking about and visualizing your happiness and success. That will put a happy look on your face. You will attract a great many people who will merely look at you because you give off that certain something everyone is seeking: confidence and happiness.

Try a simple experiment the next time you go out. Try to find a bench; maybe a park bench or a bus stop. Sit where you can see people walking up and down the street. This is the age-old pastime of people watching. Watch to see which people grab your attention. What is it about them? You will find that those who are walking confidently, dressed well and looking happy will grab your attention in a positive way. Of course, grumpy and disheveled people will also attract your attention, but in a negative way. Learn from what you see in others. Take note of celebrities, politicians and everyone in the public eye. If you want to be in the business of being noticed, change the way you walk and walk confidently! As with all traits and skills, make the conscious decision to change and improve upon them and then practice, practice, practice!

INTRODUCTIONS- THE HANDSHAKE AND GREETING

Now that you've made your entrance, keep wearing that happy expression by always thinking about and visualizing happy things. Keep your posture in order. Walk around the perimeter of the room with confidence. People will notice you. In your mind, imagine people looking at you wanting to know who you are. Although you will be dressed professionally, it is not about the clothes you wear or the expensive jewelry you adorn. It is the confidence and the happiness you exude that attracts people. Subconsciously, you are advertising that you possess what everyone else is seeking.

As you make your way around the room, you will find that you are making eye contact with others. As you look at them and they look at you, you should notice they are smiling back at you. If you are within a few steps of the person, walk up and introduce yourself, as long as you are not interrupting them.

There is no magic or secret to introducing yourself to others. It remains, though, the source of great fear for most people. It is not so much because they are afraid to introduce themselves; rather, it is because they do not know what to do afterward. In other words, it is the people who do not know how to make conversation that are hesitant to take that initial first step. Never forget that each person you meet could lead to new business, a new job or an opportunity for advancement in your career. In this next section, we are going to cover each aspect of the introduction/conversation, beginning with the handshake.

THE HANDSHAKE

The handshake is one of oldest and most symbolic of human traditions. Its roots go back thousands of years. There are several stories about its origins; some of which date back to the days of hunters and gatherers when an open hand symbolized peace in that an open hand holds no weapon. The modern idea of the handshake can be dated to the fifth century BC in ancient Greece where pottery and relics have been found with soldiers and others engaging in the handshake. As the centuries evolved, the handshake took on different meanings in various cultures. For our discussion, we will focus upon its use and meaning in Western culture.

A handshake is used in a great many instances and circumstances. For instance, when we meet someone, we shake their hand. We shake hands when we greet and when we depart from someone; we shake hands to offer congratulations, condolences, to express appreciation or to make an agreement. Athletes shake hands in a show of good sportsmanship. Politicians shake hands in a public show of good character and trust. Even enemies, when in public, are expected to shake hands and demonstrate a show of good faith.

There is a right way to shake hands and a wrong way. Young people, especially, have their own unique styles of handshaking. Whether it is the fist-pump, the three fingered- over the top— sliding pass-through—or a host of other unique handshakes, it is important that everyone know how to shake hands properly so that when the need arises you can do so with confidence.

Firstly, a handshake shows equality. When we meet someone, we are not to attempt to use a handshake to show arrogance, superiority or ego. That will not get you very far in a business relationship. Instead, your hand should be extended outward with your four fingers together and your thumb up. Your hand should be perpendicular to the floor. In this culture, we shake hands with our right hand—even if we are left handed. The only exception to this is if we are handicapped or do not have use of our right hand.

Because we shake hands with our right hand, we want to step into the handshake with our right foot forward. Don't stand at attention like a soldier. As you extend your right hand, you should step into the handshake with your right foot at the same time. Practice this motion and it will become natural for you.

Keep in mind that as you are moving in with your hand and stepping into the handshake, you are keeping eye contact with the other person while smiling. Your hand should meet the other person's hand where the thumb and the forefinger meet. Once your hands meet at that spot, you both close your grip. Your grip should be around the other person's hand and theirs around yours. Your grip should be firm, but not painful. In fact, you should use proper discretion in how firm your grip should be. For instance, if you are shaking an elderly person's hand, you will obviously want to be careful so as to not hurt them.

As you grip each other's hand, you should immediately be introducing yourself. For instance, in my case, I would step into the handshake, maintain eye contact with a smile and, upon gripping the other's hand, say, "Hi. I'm Brian Haggerty. It's a pleasure to meet you." Once the first person has introduced themselves, the second person should then say, "Hello Brian. I'm John Smith. It's a pleasure to meet you, too!" I would then repeat the other person's name and say, "So nice to meet you, John." It is very important to repeat the other person's name. Doing so helps you to remember the name. How many times have you met someone only to forget their name the instant you hear it? That is very common. But it's also embarrassing. To avoid that, repeat their name and try to make a mental note; draw a mental picture to associate it with something in your mind. In business, especially, it is very important to remember everyone's name whom you meet.

As each is making his or her introduction, the handshake is generally moving up and down about four times within a range of approximately three to four inches. The motion of your hand should come from your elbow, not the hand itself. Then, the moment each has introduced his or herself, let go! Here is where the importance of the 'right foot forward' comes into play. As you retreat back to your regular stance, you will notice that you have the perfect amount of personal space between each person. It is one thing to lean in when meeting, but once the engagement of meeting is completed, people will prefer to be within their personal space. This motion makes it completely natural and easy to accomplish for both people. Therefore, as you pull your hand and arm back toward you, you are also pulling your right leg back into your normal stance.

THE CONVERSATION

Now that you've introduced yourselves to one another, it's time to have a conversation. It is this next step that scares so many. Short of talking about the weather, most people do not know how to start and carry a conversation. It's actually quite easy, but before I explain the mechanics of a conversation, let me explain what a conversation is not.

A conversation is not your opportunity to tell your life story. Have you ever met someone who then breaks into their autobiography starting with birth and leading up to the current day? It's murderous, isn't it? You become an instant audience at the recitation of their life and times. Well, if you are going to be successful and you want people to desire your company, you must become aware of the fact that no one is interested in your life story—at least not now. You most definitely do not want to develop the reputation of being an incessant talker. That's a way to guarantee that everyone in the room will be doing their best to avoid you.

A conversation is a balanced, back and forth, question and answer session whose main purpose is to find common ground. In other words, you are looking to see what things you have in common with one another, such as common friends, hobbies, schools, businesses, interests, sports, music, etc. Have you ever noticed that when you do have a conversation with someone about a common interest that the conversation flows smoothly, easily and loses all sense of time? Exactly. That is the point. But to get to that point, you need to understand the simple mechanics of conversation.

Immediately after you and the other person have shaken hands and introduced yourselves to one another, it is time to roll directly into the conversation. The first rule to remember is to always demonstrate more interest in the other person and not talk about yourself. You can do this by asking questions. Every question requires an answer, so the act of asking questions of the other is the perfect way to start a conversation.

However, what question should you ask?

Well, that depends upon the setting of where you are. For instance, let's say you are at a wedding and you introduce yourself to someone. The first obvious question that should come to mind is, "Are you a friend of the bride or the groom?" Even if the answer is, "I am a friend of both," it is an answer. From that, you can immediately build the conversation by starting or waiting for them to ask you the same. The next order of questioning would be to talk about how you know the bride, groom or both. That brings up questions about where you live, where you work, where you went to school, etc. It is truly easy to see how a conversation can flow once you understand to ask questions that can begin with the setting of where you are.

In business, it's actually far easier to have a conversation because the obvious topic of conversation is business. An example would be a business networking luncheon or dinner. The obvious first question to ask in a conversation at a business venue would be, "What line of work are you in?" You want to find commonality in things such as: Do you both work in a sector in which you can network together? Do you work with or know the same people? Perhaps you each provide a service which each can use. In any event, a good conversation is one that goes back and forth between both people. One asks a question, the other answers and then asks another question. The moment you find commonality, you will know it immediately. From then on, the conversation flows naturally.

Sometimes, knowing how to end a conversation is equally as much a struggle for people as it is to begin one. There is no guarantee that every time you meet someone you will have a stellar conversation. But, in order to meet as many people in life as possible, we will have to have a great many conversations. Some may prove to be of little interest. However, you should always be polite to everyone and not seem rude- even if you find the conversation to be of little interest. After all, there may be times when you meet people who may find what you have to say to be of little interest. If that is the case, you would hope people would show the same degree of politeness toward you.

If, after a few minutes of speaking to someone, you decide that there is little or no ground on which to build a relationship, it is best to remain polite and to end the conversation nicely by extending your hand again and saying to the person, "Well, it was very nice to meet you. I hope to see you again some time." Ending a conversation respectfully always leaves a door open for future opportunities. But, more important, you demonstrate to the other person that you are someone who is respectful, kind and polite. It is most important to always be polite and to leave the person with a good impression of you. Who knows, perhaps that person may recommend you or your services to another.

OFFERING AND EXCHANGING BUSINESS CARDS

In business, the best way to end your conversation is to offer your business card. In fact, a true professional is very adept at the exchange of a business card. The best way to bring your conversation to a close and leave the door open for future opportunities is to ask the person with whom you are speaking for their business card. Better to ask them first than to whip yours out and offer yours. While the person is retrieving their card, you will do the same. Remember that your business card is a reflection of you. It should be clean and crisp. Don't keep them in your wallet in your back pocket where the ends may get frayed. Get yourself a nice business card holder in which your cards can be stored and always be in pristine condition. Also, to truly look professional, make sure your business cards are up to date. Don't have cards on which you have had to write in your new cell phone number or e-mail address. Make sure all of your contact information is accurate. And, most important, never give a connection more than one card unless they've asked for them. Offering someone a stack of cards is intimating that you expect them to market your services. Perhaps they may very well wish to do so, but that decision should be left to them. If they like your services so much that they will, indeed, offer them to others, they will ask you for additional cards.

When you hand your card to someone, make sure your name is facing them as they receive it. You don't want your card to be upside down. You want the recipient to be able to read your name immediately. When you receive another's card, be sure to turn it over and check the back, as well. Many cards today have logos or other information on the back of the card. Another important thing to do is to be sure you comment on the card. Perhaps the logo is interesting or eye catching. The design may be good, as well. Whatever the case, never receive one's business card and immediately put it into your pocket or holder. Read it, comment on it and be sure to thank them for it. You never know what opportunities for business may arise from the most seemingly innocuous of meetings. Everyone is a prospective opportunity—even if it is not them personally. But everyone knows other people and someone somewhere may need your services. This is why it is so important to always be gracious, kind, respectful, well-dressed and engaging when meeting someone. The more people you meet, the better and larger your circle of opportunity in business will be.

MAKING INTRODUCTIONS TO OTHERS

A truly sophisticated professional not only knows how to meet and converse with new people, she or he also knows how to introduce people to one another. If you really want to take your career up a notch and stand out, this is the skill that separates the professionals from the amateurs.

Making introductions is an art form that does follow certain rules of protocol. For instance, when introducing two people to one another, whose name is mentioned first? Very simply, it is the more important person of the two. Now I realize this is difficult to ascertain—especially in terms of knowing how to properly rank someone's importance. Since this book is primarily about business, then let's focus upon just that. It is very easy to learn how to rank people in business. First of all, in any business, the most important person of rank will always be the customer or client. After all, you are in business to serve their needs or provide a product. Therefore, even if the CEO is in the room and you wish to introduce her or him to someone who happens to be a customer or client of the company, they are the most important and, therefore, their name is mentioned first. For example, let's imagine that you are with a client of yours and your boss walks up to you. Even though your boss outranks you at the company, the client outranks the boss. Assume that your client's name is Harold Cunningham and your boss's name is Mary Winters. In order to introduce your boss, you would first say, "Mr. Cunningham, (the client) this is Mary Winters, my manager." You must always edify the person of higher rank—the person who is considered more important—by mentioning her or his name first.

Another situation may find you at a company party. At this party are all of the company employees, staff and executives. If no customers or clients are present, then you would revert to the rank within the corporate ladder. So, if you were speaking to Carol Landers of payroll and one of the vice presidents were to walk up to you, the vice-president is obviously the person of higher rank. Therefore, you mention her or his name first. Let's say the vice president is Peter Lawrence. You would say, "Mr. Lawrence, this is Carol Landers who works in payroll."

But you are still not finished. If the two people you are introducing do not know each other, then you want to be able to offer some information on each person so the other knows who they are, what they do and may, if they choose, have a conversation. Remember to always be seeking commonality. This skill is important not only in business, but anywhere in life. You may very well be the host of an event. As the host, you will be very busy introducing people to one another. When you do, knowing how to point out some common ground between the two is a very valuable skill and will help people to get to know one another. By assisting people in starting a conversation, you help them feel comfortable. And once you have done this, you can move on to make more introductions.

A very important thing to keep in mind in business is that you should know when it is appropriate to have a conversation. Sometimes, just shaking hands and meeting someone is enough. For example, if you are introduced by someone to the president of the company, and you are down on the corporate totem pole, you should not see this as an opportunity to start asking her or him questions or making suggestions as to how to better run the company. Doing so runs a great risk of your seeming silly and immature and certainly not professional or sophisticated. If the person of higher rank wishes to engage with you or someone else, that is their decision. Allow them to decide whether or not to engage in a conversation. Further, you must defer to them to lead the conversation and ask questions. If your opinion on something is asked, that is fine to offer it. However, unless your opinion is asked, never offer it to someone who is higher in rank than you. Don't ramble and do not ask personal questions of them. You want to leave them with a positive opinion of you, not a "Who is this person and why are they speaking to me?" question in their mind.

PERSONAL SPACE

Regardless of the caliber of the conversation with another, you will want to become aware of personal space. No one likes to have someone standing too close or towering over them. Therefore, make sure you are aware of this at all times. If you are ever speaking to someone and you notice the person steps away from you, they are sending a signal that you are in their personal space. Don't attempt to close the space by stepping toward them. Instead, keep a person at arm's length and remember the rule of shaking hands. When you first shake someone's hand, you put your right foot forward. When you let go of the person's hand and resume to a normal stance, you will be at the perfect distance from that person to respect their personal space. Imagine if you were meeting a prospective client for the first time. The last thing you want to do is to make them feel uncomfortable or violated of their personal space. Making someone uncomfortable is not a good approach toward winning their business or account. What's most important is making them feel comfortable and in control—at all times—of themselves and their surroundings.

Sometimes you may be meeting with a client or higher ranking member of your company in a very crowded space. You may not have the sufficient distance even after you resume your stance to allow for personal space. When this happens, stand shoulder to shoulder with the person. By standing shoulder to shoulder, you can speak to them from the side. This helps in a crowded, loud room because you will in essence be able to speak into their right or left ear— depending upon what side of the person by whom you are standing. When doing so, you are still close to them, but you are not standing directly in front of them. This stance will allow both of you to feel at ease without one or the other feeling confined. Failing to do so or causing them any level of discomfort can cost you their business.

I have been around many people throughout my years in business and politics who are definitely not aware of personal space issues. Some people wind up giving you the Johnson treatment— named after President Lyndon Johnson's notorious use of his imposing, physical size to stand over people in order to intimidate them. You never want to intimidate anyone—much less a client, customer, co-worker or manager when you are speaking to them. Doing so will guarantee that they will not wish to be in your company ever again. Remember, people will not tell you this. You have to be aware of it yourself and make sure that at all times you are making everyone around you feel comfortable. You want people to like you and to wish to get to know you. Respecting people's personal space is very important in our ability to develop solid, long-lasting relationships in business. In addition, a boss or manager is not likely to recommend you for advancement, if she or he feels that you lack the people skills so needed in attaining, building or acquiring new business and customers.

BODY LANGUAGE

When we do speak to others, we should always be expressing body language, which shows that we are interested in what they have to say. Even if you are not very interested, it is, as I said, important to show the proper respect. You should always point your chest and feet toward the person who is speaking and maintain a healthy eye contact. This does not mean you should stare at them, either. Staring can also be very intimidating. Good eye contact means holding your gaze at the space between their eyes and, every few seconds, moving your eyes around so as to avoid staring. Our body language speaks more loudly than what we say in many cases. You don't want to be checking your watch, you absolutely do not want to be looking at your mobile device and you should not fidget with things in your pocket. If a prospective client is telling you what she or he is expecting of your company or services, the wrong body language can signal to them that you do not care about what they have to say. Good listening skills are paramount when dealing with people in business. A good listener is one who uses both body language and facial expression to show the person that we are attentive to what they are saying. It is a skill and, like all skills, it requires practice. If you want to develop your people skills and earn the respect of others in business, you must be gracious to everyone. If you took the time to introduce yourself, then you need to stay the course and show respect throughout the conversation. Further, in business, you must give one hundred percent of your attention—for as long as it takes—while a customer, client or person of higher rank is speaking with you. This is what will help you make wonderful new friendships and connections throughout your business or professional life. Make people comfortable, smile, give them your attention and you will do very well in fostering new business relationships. You will earn the respect of your co-workers, boss, manager and everyone else you encounter within your professional life.

SURROUND YOURSELF WITH SUCCESSFUL PEOPLE

People have always asked the proverbial question, "What can I do to become successful?" While there is no single secret and certainly no exact road map for success, one of the easiest things you can do is to surround yourself with people who are already successful and more successful than you. The company we keep usually rubs off on us. If you are always hanging around with negative people, such as those who use vulgarity, who hold prejudicial beliefs or are sloppy in their appearance, this behavior will absolutely influence the way you act and behave. While I don't say you should abandon all of your friends if they act or carry themselves like this, I do highly recommend that you start to associate with people who have goals, dreams, ambitions and desires for success—as well as those who are already successful.

Suppose you are in sales? With whom should you be associating more—the top sales person or the lowest? Obviously, you would want to be with the person who has achieved the greatest level of success and continues to do so continuously. Successfully minded people have their minds on success, they talk about success and everything they do is geared toward their individual success. When you surround yourself with successful people, you will feel successful. Your conversation will always be about success. Speak successfully, act successfully and dress successfully. Dressing successfully means that you should be in the proper attire for the occasion. After all, if you are meeting other successful people at a casual restaurant, you still should not be casual as the public views casual. You should be in business casual which, for men, means you should be wearing slacks or khakis, a shirt with a collar, nice shoes and a well-shaven appearance. For women, it means a skirt should be no shorter than at the knee. The neckline should be high and shoulders should not be exposed. Shoes should be leather heeled.

Regardless if you are a man or woman, you should always err on the side of the classic look and avoid trendy clothing or clothes with bright colors that will attract too much attention. It is best to dress more conservatively than to attempt to be cutting-edge.

Make sure you know exactly what your company's policy is toward attire. Check your human resources' handbook. It will generally outline, in detail, exactly what is expected for your attire. You will do best if you always seek to dress well and be neat and clean in your appearance. If you have tattoos, cover them. The better your attire and style of dress, the more successful you will appear and feel.

CHAPTER THREE

Communication

When we act the part and dress the part in business, we are on our way to establishing a solid reputation that will help us to grow and be successful in all we do. But, merely acting and dressing the part is not the whole picture. What truly sets us apart and establishes our reputation is how we communicate. Communication comes in many forms. It is composed of both verbal and non-verbal communication, including grammar and word usage, vocabulary, as well as our written communication, in both traditional and social media outlets.

Like all personal skills, the ability to be well spoken along with effective communication skills is a choice we each make. While people do assess our level of intelligence on how we speak and communicate, we do not require great intellect in order to improve upon these skills. All we need to do is to make the decision to learn, practice and incorporate these skills into our communications. If you are truly seeking success in your business or career, the improvement of your communication skills is a fundamental aspect of your personal brand. According to a survey by the National Association of Colleges and Employers (NACE), the number one skill a prospective employer seeks in a prospective employee is the ability to communicate.

Developing good communication skills is paramount to your success. Studies have consistently shown that people who are well-spoken earn more money, command more respect and appear more intelligent. Having a great resume is one thing—for anyone

---

Communication Skills and Team Work Rank #1 with Prospective Employers.

What sets two equally qualified job candidates apart can be as simple as who has the better communication skills. An annual survey of the job market for new college graduates shows that, year after year, certain skills, attributes, and qualities show up on employers' "most wanted" list. According to the Job Outlook 2013 *report, published by the National Association of Colleges and Employers (NACE), after confirming the requisite major and course work for the job, employers screen candidates by GPA (grade point average) and relevant work experience—often earned during college years through internships or cooperative education assignments. "Just over 78 percent of employers screen candidates by GPA," says Marilyn Mackes, NACE's executive director. "Also important is related work experience. Less than 5 percent of employers say that work experience doesn't factor into their hiring decisions." What makes a new graduate stand out from equally qualified competitors, however, is evidence of the "soft skills" needed in the workplace. Employers prize skills such as communication skills, the ability to work in a team, and problem-solving skills.*

Moral of the story*: Communicate and work well, earn well!*

Source: National Association of Colleges and Employers

Site source: naceweb.org

---

can look good on paper. But when we arrive for an interview in the appropriate dress and with a good presentation, the way we speak and express ourselves is what will ultimately get us the job.

But before you fear having to return to the good old days of grade school and having to learn your grammar and word usage all over again, the good news is that you do not have to rehash what you learned years ago. Developing and improving upon your communication skills can be accomplished simply by choosing to do so and taking the time to learn and practice these skills. The principles of good communication are universal and do not require an advanced degree. Make the decision right now to monitor everything you say, all that you write and the manner in which you express yourself and you will find that with a little effort, you will become a better communicator. It is a process that will continue throughout your career and whose mastery will most definitely make you a greater success in business.

HOW TO SOUND AND SEEM MORE INTELLIGENT

"A fool and his words are soon parted."

—*William Shenstone*

Before we begin any discussion about our grammar and word usage, it is necessary to learn the simple principles of communication, which underscore everything we say. Just sounding more intelligent is enough to cause us to appear more intelligent. We can actually improve our communication skills and come across as more intelligent just by learning some basic principles.

1.   LESS IS MORE

When it comes to talking, most of us are quite adept. Everyone has an opinion, and most are very fast to offer it. But when it comes to being an effective communicator in business and portraying ourselves as intelligent, thoughtful individuals who offer words that are chosen very carefully and expressed in a manner most efficiently, many fall short. Often, it is not what we say, but how we say it. And the number of words we use, if too many, devalue what we are saying. In business, time is money. People have little time to waste. Someone who rambles on and gives no thought to what she or he says can only diminish her or himself in the eyes of their peers. They may be seen as foolish and ignorant. So the first thing you will want to do is to create a filter for all of your words. There is no need to always say something. And you definitely do not want to say the first thing that pops into your head. The less you say, the more of an impact your words will have when you say them.

The greatest skill you can develop is to become a better listener. Listening allows for you to collect information from others so that your response is a direct answer to someone's question or offers information that enhances the conversation. If you make less of yourself when you speak with others, they will always wind up asking you more and placing a higher value on your opinion. Therefore, never monopolize a conversation. Don't talk about yourself. Be sure that the words you offer are relevant to what is being discussed. For instance, if you are being interviewed for a job, and the interviewer asks you to tell them a little about yourself, this is not an opening for your life story. Instead, you will use this as an opportunity to reveal your skills, areas of expertise and your background—only with regard to how all of it would apply to the job you are seeking and how you can enhance the prospective company with what you bring to the table.

As you begin to develop the reputation for being someone who doesn't talk nonsense, doesn't ramble on and on about yourself and only speaks to the matter at hand, your opinions will become far more valuable to others and your words will be far more poignant. So begin to filter everything that comes out of your mouth. Make sure you say as much as you can with as few words as possible!

2. PAUSE AND THINK BEFORE YOU SPEAK

Don't be so quick to open your mouth. Taking a second to pause before you answer someone actually allows for you to choose and formulate your words and response. It demonstrates intellect and thoughtfulness. It is a sign that you give thought to what you say and are not so fast to ramble or offer a nonsensical response to someone. This will help you to develop your filter so that nothing slips out of your mouth that shouldn't. Speak slowly. Perhaps it is best to avoid an abundance of caffeine or sugar before you will be in a position to speak at a meeting as they will make you nervous and far more likely to spew your words in a quick fashion. A short, split second pause before each sentence is all that you need to apply a filter to your words to choose them wisely.

3. ASK QUESTIONS

People are afraid to ask questions. They fear that if they ask a question, they come across as being ignorant or even stupid. There is a saying which says that the only stupid question is the one that is not asked. No one knows everything. No one is expected to know everything. Asking a question does not make you appear as if you are less intelligent. In fact, it shows that you are intelligent and humble enough to recognize what you do not know on a given subject. It shows that you are giving serious thought to something and respect others enough to provide you with information that will ultimately allow you to formulate a well-thought response. In addition, it will guarantee that your answer is exactly what the person is seeking. Maybe the question was not clear. Never fear a follow up question in order to clarify what the other person is asking. The better you understand the question, the more direct and comprehensive your answer.

> ## *Good Communication Skills = More money and Greater Upward Mobility!*
>
> *In 2010, a Korn/Ferry study conducted at McGladrey—a national consulting firm—assessed the capabilities of employees classified as high potentials as assessed by their managers. The top five items were communication-related. The ability to convey ideas and information accurately and effectively, along with the ability to influence and persuade others, are key attributes of employees who successfully move up in an organization.*
>
> ***Moral of the story****: Improving your communication skills puts money in your bank account!*
>
> *Source: eHow.com Author: Leigh Richards*
> *Survey: Korn/Ferry International*

4.   DON'T PORTRAY YOUR OPINION AS FACT

We live in a world where everyone has their own opinion. Social media and message boards are chock full of every opinion on each and every subject there is. The problem is that most people do not understand the difference between their opinions versus facts. Herein is one of the greatest traps you can set for yourself in business, if you are not careful and not aware of this snare. One of the fastest and surest ways of being embarrassed in a business setting is to have someone call you out on something you state, as if it is fact without stating it as an opinion. There is no wrong in sharing your opinion. But make sure that you always clarify that you are offering your opinion when you do.

5. FEAR NOT THE ONE WORD RESPONSE

Many times, the answer to a question is a yes or a no. But how often have we heard people being asked a yes or no question, only to appear evasive in their response by going into a diatribe that seems designed to evade the question. If the response to a question is a yes or a no, then begin your answer with the appropriate reply. Then, if you feel the need to expand upon your answer with an explanation, do so after you have given your yes or no. Not only will this be greatly appreciated, but it will show others that you are truthful, confident and direct—each of which is vital to your success and reputation in business. It will certainly impress the boss or higher-ups if they know you to be someone who gives a direct answer.

6. SPEAK CLEARLY

There's nothing worse than someone who mumbles or who cannot be heard by others at the same table. If you are someone who speaks quietly, or mumbles, or both, then start to speak with a little more confidence and turn up the volume. While you shouldn't shout, speaking clearly will demonstrate confidence in what you are saying. Everyone appreciates someone who speaks clearly. Keep your hands away from your mouth and make eye contact while looking around at the people with you when you speak. Make sure you are articulate and are fully pronouncing your words. Do not use slang and avoid colloquialisms that may only be known to you and not the others who are present.

GRAMMAR

In addition to incorporating the above principles of communication, the usage of good grammar is vital. It adds to our perceived level of intelligence and demonstrates an attention to detail—two extremely important factors in business. Grammar as a subject is not taught in today's schools like it once was. Neither is its importance upheld by society like it was in years past. But just because most people fall down the slippery-slope of sloppy grammatical goo does not mean that it is any less important in business today than ever before. The good news for you is that if you actually work at improving your grammar and word usage, you will be among the select few and will stand out from the crowd. Those who seek to rise up within the echelon of the business world must have good grammar and word usage.

Children learn how to speak long before they learn how to read. They learn how to speak by hearing and imitating the sounds they hear. The same goes for anyone who wishes to improve upon their grammar. You don't have to worry about returning to grammar school to learn the grammatical terms and academic principles of grammar. You can easily learn to speak with good grammar by making the choice to do it and then consciously becoming aware of your grammar and correcting yourself as you do. Within a short period of time, speaking with proper grammar will become as much a habit as once speaking incorrectly.

The use of good grammar is important in both our verbal and written communication. Its usage in business is vital if you are seeking to advance yourself. Below is a list of the most common grammatical errors people make. While by no means exhaustive, it will help you to identify the correct usage in everyday language and will help you to get started in improving your grammar and word usage.

THE MOST COMMON GRAMMATICAL ERRORS PEOPLE MAKE

1. IS IT "I" OR IS IT "ME?"

Yes. That is the question. The number one most common grammatical error is the misuse of the pronouns "I" and "me." It is the most commonly made error because we refer to ourselves more each day than to anything else. If you learn one lesson in grammar in this section, this should be it.

"I" is always the subject of a sentence. *I am going to the store. I like pizza. I need a vacation, etc.*

"Me" is always the object of a sentence. *Give that to me. Are you coming with me? She wrote a song about me.*

When we are only speaking about ourselves, we generally use the right pronoun. But the problem begins whenever we add someone else to the sentence. All of sudden, people say "Me" when they should say "I" and "I" when they should say "me."

For instance, if I am going to a meeting and Maria is coming with me, all of sudden I say: *"Maria and me are going to the meeting."* Well let me ask you this—if I take Maria's name out of the previous sentence, would I say *"Me am going to the meeting"*? I am sure I wouldn't. So why, then, does most everyone change "I" to "me" when someone else is added to the subject? No matter if it is Maria, a gaggle of geese or the whole free world, as long as you are the subject of the sentence (The one doing, saying, going or engaging in any action), the correct pronoun is always "I."

On the other hand, when it comes to using the right objective pronoun, the same thing happens. Again, when we are alone in the sentence, we get it correct as in, *"Kevin issued his monthly report to me."* But, add another person to the sentence and all of a sudden, I say, *"Kevin issued his monthly report to Maria and I."* Take out Maria's name. Would you say, *"Kevin issued his monthly report* to I"? Maybe Bob Marley would sing it like that, but I don't think you would use it in a sentence. The correct way to say it is, *"Kevin issued his monthly report to Maria and me."*

The easiest way to make sure you are using the correct pronoun is to remove the other person (or persons) from the sentence and see if it sounds correct. Once you've done that, you will know you are saying it correctly. This will take some time to fix if you've been making this mistake a long time. But becoming aware of it and using the "remove the other" tactic will help you to get it right. If you are giving a presentation to a board of directors, you don't want to embarrass yourself by using the wrong pronoun. Doing so shows sloppiness. Further, in my own case, I find it to devalue the information being offered because how accurate are the details if a person does not show the attention to the details of his or her grammar?

2. LIE VERSUS LAY

How many times have you been tired and have said, *"I am going to lay down"*? Guess what? You've been saying it wrong. While this can get confusing, lie and lay have two distinct meanings.

Lie means to "rest or recline."

Lay means to "put or place."

So, when you are tired, you would say that you are *"going to lie down"* (rest; recline). But if you set the dinner table, you will *"lay the forks and knives"* (put or place).

Where people really get jammed-up in the lie v. lay conundrum is when using the different tenses. For instance, the tenses of each are listed below:

Lie, lying, lay, lain

Lay, laying, laid, laid

As you see, the past-tense of lie is lay. But while confusing on the surface, you can know which to use by its usage in the sentence. Here are sentences which contain examples of the usage for each:

Lie: *I am going to lie down. My sister is lying in the sun. When I was sick, I lay in bed all day. Grandma has lain on the couch all day with a bad cold.*

Lay: *Our manager held a meeting to lay the ground work for the new initiative. I am laying the foundation for our new sales plan. At today's meeting, I laid out my concerns about the new company policies. The sales department had laid out their strategy to achieve the new goals for October.*

While it will take you some time to master all of the different tenses for lie and lay, the one you should remember is that you never "lay down" when tired, you "lie down." Learning the proper way to use lie and lay will put you in a very unique and exclusive group of people. So, to make the greatest impression in business and to rise up, take the time to learn this. It will be well worth it for your career.

3.   ENDING A SENTENCE WITH A PREPOSITION

If you truly wish to speak impressively, this is the section that separates the amateurs from the pros. She or he who ends a sentence with a preposition speaks incorrectly. It is not difficult to learn how to stop ending a sentence with prepositions. It only requires some diligent practice and listening skills to hear and identify the correct way to speak.

First, let's take a look at prepositions and what they are:

A preposition is a little word which represents position, location, direction, etc. Examples of prepositions are: *Above, Below, Among,*

Between, In, Toward, Along, Through, At, Behind, Beside, For, In, Into, etc.

A preposition usually indicates the temporal, spatial or logical relationship of its object to the rest of the sentence, i.e., its location. Some examples:

- The reports are **on** the table.

- Your paycheck is **in** the mail.

- My report will run **through** the necessary channels.

- We are headed **toward** profitability.

Prepositions are used to link nouns, pronouns or phrases to other words in a sentence. Therefore, a preposition cannot be the last word in a sentence, for then there would be no word with which it can be joined.

It is rare today to hear someone speak who does not end a sentence with a preposition. Though the rules in daily conversation have eased on this as well, it is worth learning and knowing so you may speak properly and impressively, if needed. It is most certainly used in proper writing.

First, let's look at examples of **incorrectly** ending a sentence with a preposition:

- This is the entrance I came in <u>through.</u>

- This is the book I am interested <u>in</u>.

- That's a great club to be associated <u>with.</u>

- This is the direction we were going <u>toward.</u>

- He is the person I need to talk <u>to.</u>

As you can see, the above all sound normal and correct. However, they each end with a preposition, which is not grammatically correct. Now let us look at the same sentences written the proper way:

- This is the entrance <u>through</u> which I came.

- This is the book <u>in</u> which I am interested.

- That's a great club <u>with</u> which to be associated.

- This is the direction <u>toward</u> which we were going.

- He is the person <u>to</u> whom I need to speak.

I am sure you have heard someone say, "Who am I speaking to?" on the phone. But the correct sentence is, "With whom am I speaking?" Again, you do not need to live or die by this rule in your daily conversations. However, understanding this rule and applying it to your speaking or writing only serves to edify your speaking skills and level of intelligence. It's rarely used in general conversation anymore. But, if you are speaking in business or giving a presentation in front of a board of directors, you would make a very great impression when following this rule. And if not speaking, you would be most impressive if you were to incorporate the proper form in your writing.

4. HUNG V. HANGED

This common mistake is made by most everyone. Simply put, any object such as a coat, a hat or a picture is "hung." *The man <u>hung</u> his coat and hat when he arrived for the meeting.* However, when referring to a person, it is said they were "hanged." *Saddam Hussein was <u>hanged</u> for his crimes against humanity.*

5. "I COULD 'CARE' LESS"

This expression is used countless times each day by most people. The problem is that most say it incorrectly. When you don't care in the least about something, you should say, *"I couldn't (or could not) care less.* If you "could" care less, then you are saying that there is actually less caring you can do.

6. "WELL" V. "GOOD"

Two words which are horribly misused are "well" and "good." "Well" is both an adverb, e.g., "He is well spoken" or "She is well dressed" and is also an adjective, e.g., "I am well" or "She is well."

"Good" is both an adjective, e.g., "A good job" or "A good book" and a noun, e.g., "The greatest *good* is helping others."

The next time someone asks you how you did on a sales call or at a presentation, you should say: *"I did well, thank you!"*

7. "WOULD OF, SHOULD OF, COULD OF"

This is pure sloppiness on the part of those who use these elements of slang. The correct usage is *would have, should have, could have.* For instance, *you would have been able to know this if you read the company's report. You should have read it by now. If you did, you could have recognized this error a long time ago.* While it may not be apparent when you say these words, it will most certainly be apparent when you write them. The last thing you want to do is use *would of, should of, could of* when writing or speaking in the business or professional world.

8. "EITHER OR; NEITHER NOR"

"Neither" is a singular adjective and can only be paired with "nor" in a sentence. "Neither" is never paired with "or." When using "neither" in a sentence, you are saying not the first object and not the second object. The nouns/pronouns are not in agreement with one another, e.g. *John nor Sue is going to the training seminar.* In this example, neither the first object (John) nor the second object (Sue) is going to the seminar. Remember, neither is singular so you would never say, "*Neither John nor Sue ARE going to the seminar.*"

"Either" is also a singular adjective. It means one or the other, but not both. "Either" expresses one noun/pronoun doing one thing and the other noun/pronoun doing another; in this way it is a "positive" word because what is occurring is true. "Either" can be paired with "or" but not "nor." For example, *either* John or Sue <u>is</u> going to the training seminar tonight. In this example, one or the other will be going- not both.

If the subjects are both plural, then the verb would be plural. For example, *either* the Smiths *or* the Jacksons <u>are</u> attending tonight's meeting. Here, the subjects (The Smiths and the Jacksons) represent more than one person. Therefore, because the subjects are both plural, you would use the verb <u>are.</u>

Here is where it can get tricky, but is actually easy once you practice it. If one subject is plural and the other singular, you would use the verb tense that reflects the subject closest to the verb. For example, *neither* the executives *nor* Mr. Jones <u>is</u> attending the meeting this evening. The "executives" are plural, but Mr. Jones is singular and is closest to the verb and would therefore call for a singular verb of <u>is</u> as opposed to <u>are.</u> Conversely, the opposite would be true, if the subject closest to the verb is plural, but the first subject is singular. For example, *neither* Mr. Jones *nor* the executives <u>are</u> attending the meeting tonight. "Executives" is plural, so the verb would be <u>are.</u>

9. LESS V. FEWER

Once you understand the difference, these two are easy. *Less* refers to "Quantity" while *fewer* refers to "Number"; e.g., John had far <u>less</u> work to do this month. In this case, less refers to the quantity of work John had to do. The quantity of work John had to do was less than it was previously.

"Fewer," on the other hand, refers to a number. Because John had less work this month, he needed <u>fewer</u> supplies. In this case, "fewer" refers to the number of supplies John needed.

10. CAN V. MAY

Simply put, <u>can</u> indicates the ability to do something, while <u>may</u> indicates permission to do it. For instance, you would NOT say, "<u>Can</u> *I have a look at our sales figures*?" This would indicate you're asking if you have the ability to have a look at the figures. What you would say is, "<u>May</u> *I have a look at our sales figures*?" You can say, "*I* <u>can</u> *reach our monthly goal of one hundred new accounts*" because you are signifying your ability to do so.

REMINDERS

The examples above are a mere sliver of the most common mistakes in word usage, pronunciation and expression. While I do a great amount of teaching on this subject, I wanted you to at least become aware of those which are used most by people in daily conversation. Using good grammar is very important, if you want to be taken seriously in business.

We have a great amount of slang in today's language such as *my bad* (meaning my mistake) or *true dat* (meaning, I agree). We use abbreviations of all sorts—especially in texts and e-mails. Just remember—you want to be able to separate your personal communications with your business communications. If while writing or speaking to your friends you wind up using slang, abbreviations or any other sort of local dialect, that's fine. But, you must be able to turn it on and off when in your professional arena, if you want to be taken seriously. In fact, you would be better off getting into the habit of using correct words and grammar at all times. We'll focus more upon e-mailing, texting and using social media later. Just remember that everything you say or write is a reflection of you and your personal brand. If you want to be a success, be mindful that everything about you reflects your professionalism and level of intelligence.

NON-VERBAL COMMUNICATION

Many times, how we communicate non-verbally can be more telling than our actual words. In business, we want to make sure that everything we portray about ourselves demonstrates approachability, openness, honesty, attentiveness and thoughtfulness. This is why it is important to become aware of what our body language and facial expression are indicating to others. When used in conjunction with our words, body language can become a great enhancement to what we say by sending forth the subconscious signals that match our words and attract people to you rather than scaring them away. Let's take a look at the most prominent of body language and the signals they send when we use them properly.

SMILE

The most potent body language that is most telling is a smile. As we discussed earlier in the book, a smile is attractive and engaging. People love those who smile because a smile represents happiness.

While it isn't appropriate to have a constant smile on your face, you should always smile when meeting or greeting someone. You can attract attention to yourself merely by smiling. If you find it hard to smile, then think about something that makes you happy and the smile will be natural and easy, as was discussed earlier.

EYE CONTACT

In Chapter One, we discussed the importance of making eye contact when meeting someone. But it is also important to maintain eye contact when speaking with someone. In fact, if you meet or are speaking with someone outdoors and are wearing sunglasses, remove them so the other person can see your eyes. Even if the conversation you are having with someone is not interesting, it is important to be polite and always keep eye contact. In business, if you do not look someone in the eye when speaking with them, you will come across as evasive or perhaps appear as if you are hiding something. Eye contact is hypnotic and powerful. People will be drawn to you if you look them in the eye.

POSTURE

Again, our posture speaks volumes about us. We can look confident or tired, weary or awake, engaged or uninterested just by our posture. Our posture is important whether we are sitting or standing. It's also important when we are walking. As we discussed earlier, the easiest way to have good posture is to keep your chin level with the ground. This will keep your head looking outward, which is how you want to show confidence. If you are always looking down at your cell phone or mobile device, as the title of this book states, you cannot have good posture and will not be able to look people in the eye or have them notice your face.

When you are speaking to someone, be sure to stand facing them. Keep good eye contact and point your feet toward the other person. If you are standing with your feet pointed in another direction or with your upper body facing somewhere else, you are sending a non-verbal clue that you are not interested in speaking with them.

Are your facial expressions and body language perfect together?

Princeton University researchers report in the Journal of Science that facial expressions can be ambiguous and subjective when viewed independently. In four separate experiments, participants more accurately guessed the pictured emotion based on body language—alone or combined with facial expressions—than on facial context alone. Senior researcher and Princeton Professor of Psychology Alexander Todorov said that these results challenge the clinical—and conventional—presumption that the face best communicates feeling. Indeed, despite the findings, a majority of the study's participants sided with the face when asked how they gauge feelings, a misconception the researchers referred to as "illusory facial affect."

Moral of the story*: Get your facial expressions and your body language in sync with one another!*

Source: Princeton.edu Article author: Morgan Kelley
Study: Body Cues, Not Facial Expressions, Discriminate Between Intense Positive and Negative Emotions.

Report: Science 30 November 2012:
Vol. 338 **no. 6111** *pp. 1225-1229*
DOI: *10.1126/science.1224313*

Avoid folding your arms in front of you across your chest. This makes you appear rigid and closed-minded. You can either clasp your hands behind your back or in front of you below your belly. This stance makes you appear "open" and "approachable." Try not to put your hands in your pockets. When you do this, you have a tendency to fidget with things in your pocket. In addition, hiding your hands is a form of concealment.

When you are seated, make sure you don't slouch in your seat. Sit up straight, put your feet on the floor and keep your eyes on the person who is speaking. You want to appear awake, alert, engaged and confident.

GAIT

Our gait is how we carry ourselves when we walk. Having good posture, as discussed above, is important when we walk. You want to have a confident, yet energetic stride. Swing your arms as you walk and don't keep them in your pockets or hanging stiffly at your sides. Keep your feet pointed straight. Keep your head up, smile and acknowledge those around you and you will send a powerful non-verbal message that you are confident and approachable. If you walk into a meeting like this, people will take notice and they will pick up on the non-verbal body language that says you are there to do business and are ready for anything.

HAND GESTURES

Our hands and the gestures we make can be a great complement to our words. But, they can also affect us negatively if we do not use them appropriately. You should never point at someone when speaking to them or when making a point to them. Try only to use your hand gestures when it is going to help you to make a point or underscore something you want the others around you to hear or remember. But don't swing them around all of the time and use them constantly. This will devalue their use when you truly want to make a point.

WRITTEN COMMUNICATION

In business, a great deal of our communication is in written form. Every word we write is a reflection of who we are and our level of intelligence and professionalism. It also represents our personal brand. In fact, it is vital that our written communication complement our verbal communication and not portray a conflicting message to others. In today's digital environment of e-mail, texting and social media, we write more than we speak. However, remember that most of our writing is in digital format. It is there for nearly all the world to read. And, in many cases, it is there forever.

E-MAIL

E-mail is the most commonly used form of communication in business today. To be a professional, you must be cognizant to whom it is you are e-mailing. Make sure that you keep your business e-mails separate from your personal e-mails. Avoid forwarding stories, off-color jokes or chain e-mails to anyone with whom you do business. Never discuss or demonstrate your stance on any social, political or religious opinions when communicating in e-mail. Don't try to use humor because—unless you are a professional comedic writer—your humor may not convey properly to the recipient.

In business, you should write your e-mails the same as if you were typing out a letter. Keep it short, on point and do not ramble. No one wants to read a long-winded e-mail. Anything in depth should be reserved for a phone or in-person conversation. Don't scare your clients or business associates away with an e-mail that needs to be scrolled down several pages. No one will read it and they will avoid reading anything you write in the future. Be concise. Respect the other person's time. Stay to the subject and stick to a few key points.

In many cases, an initial e-mail may lead to a series of back and forth e-mails on a subject. When you first e-mail someone, you should address them by their name. If you do not know the person personally, address them as Ms. or Mr. followed by their surname. Sign your full name. If the person responds by signing their first name that is the signal that you may then address them in follow up e-mails by their first name. You should do the same. Also, after several back and forth e-mails, it is common to no longer even use a name, but just to answer or offer more information about the subject. This is acceptable. After all, on your twelfth e-mail back and forth to Mr. Petersen, you don't have to keep being so formal and start off each response with "Dear Mr. Petersen."

In business, never use slang or emoticons when e-mailing unless it is with someone with whom you have developed a personal relationship. All of your e-mails should adhere to the rules of grammar and should be formatted accordingly. This is your way of communicating and demonstrating your level of professionalism. People in business will not take you seriously if you do not know how to write a professional e-mail.

Make sure you re-read and proofread your e-mails. An error can make you look sloppy, inattentive or worse—unintelligent. Beware of words that do not get flagged by spell check, but can make you seem less intelligent. Be sure to know the proper form of *their, there and they're; to, too and two; whose and who's*, as well as *its and it's*. These are words that sound alike but will not get picked up by your spell check because they are not misspelled, but are very much mistakenly misused. Again, each time you err in your word usage, you are denoting a lack of attention to detail and perhaps a lower level of intelligence. Intellect actually has nothing to do with it. It is a case of your being sloppy and not having taken the time to proof-read or learn to write correctly. Make sure you practice and learn the differences between these words and when to use them.

TEXTING

Texting is quickly becoming the fastest way to communicate. Today people text more than they e-mail. But that should not change the rules of professionalism. If you are texting back and forth with your friend or a family member and use abbreviations such as *lol, cul8r, LMAO, ttyl* or any others, that's fine. But if you text a business associate, client or co-worker with whom you do not have a familiar relationship, avoid using abbreviations or emoticons. Further, don't text long sentences and do not try to have a conversation when you text. Use texting as a means of exchanging quick snippets of information that are pertinent to business. Remember that in business even our texts represent our personal brand and level of professionalism.

FACEBOOK

Facebook: where the world tries to show the rest of the world that they have a life. I've witnessed more trouble for people in business as the result of Facebook than I have from any other social media. Facebook can be a great thing. It keeps us in touch with our family, friends and old schoolmates. It's great for sharing pictures and even for building an online audience of followers. But there is a dark side to Facebook and if you want to be successful in business, you should not cross the threshold into the dark side of the Facebook foray.

One of the first things you need to know is that some prospective employers have begun asking their job candidates to sign on to their Facebook account right there at the interview. Not fair, you say? Maybe so, but if you refuse, you will probably not get the job and there are another one hundred people who would be more than happy to do so, if it means getting that job. The reach of Facebook and its transparent venue for everything in people's lives has allowed for far too many people to forget that not everyone on Facebook is

---

Not everyone is LOLing when their boss checks their Facebook

In a recent CareerBuilder.com survey, 37% of employers are now checking a job candidate's social media profile. This number has increased exponentially in the past few years and is expected to grow more as social media becomes a larger part of our lives. According to the survey, 65 percent of employers are looking as to whether or not a candidate presents him or herself professionally online. Other reasons include investigating prospective employees' social profiles to see if they will fit in with the company's culture (51 percent), wanting to learn more about their qualifications (51 percent), to learn if they are a well-rounded individual (35 percent) and only 12 percent look for reasons not to hire someone.

***The Moral of the Story**: Keep your postings clean, kind, positive and professional!*

Source: tmprod.com
Author: Michael L. Hoffman
Survey Source: CareerBuilder.com

---

your friend. Further, posting what's on your mind is not always a good thing, if you are saying something in anger or post an opinion on any topic that may involve politics, religion or, even worse, your job or boss.

Everything you write on Facebook can and will be used against you. It seems that many people have an overwhelming need for approval. They feel that by expressing themselves on Facebook, other people actually care what they think or say. Well, the people who care most are usually the people who are looking to use something against you. There is absolutely no reason whatsoever, and no advantage to posting your deepest thoughts, most fervent opinions and craziest of photos for everyone to see. If you truly want to build your personal brand, then Facebook is actually a great way to do so—as long as you adhere to the rules that protect your reputation and image and guarantee that you will avoid embarrassment in the future.

Don't write anything that you wouldn't want on the front page of *The New York Times*. You have a political or religious opinion on something? Great! So does everyone else. Keep it to yourself and never write it or engage in one of those lovely long message threads where people say the meanest and most narrow-minded of things about someone or something. Hopefully you've figured out that your opinions do evolve over your lifetime. Would you like it if someone read something you wrote about someone or something five years ago, made an assessment about you, and yet you think differently about that same person or thing today? Don't like your boss? Don't write it. Even if she or he is not one of your Facebook friends, one of your co-workers may be. She or he may very well share it in an attempt to undermine you. The only way to completely avoid any embarrassment on Facebook is only write things which are positive, flavorful and kind. This way, no matter who reads it, or when they read it, they can only see that you are a kind, positive and thoughtful person. Nothing can ever come back to haunt you. Also, make your security settings as strict as possible. Make sure any posts or photos others may tag of you must first be approved by you. Keep tight control of your image at all times! Never reveal what you think about a person, place or thing. If you follow this rule, you'll have nothing to fear if you are asked at an interview to sign on to your Facebook. More and more employers are checking your social media posts these days. With all of the competition in the job market, don't make it easy for them to pass you over for someone else.

TWITTER

Alas! More careers have been ended in 140 characters or less thanks to the same mistakes as those with Facebook. What's worse is that tweets are searchable by search engines. While you can make your tweets private, few do because it is very difficult to manage. The bottom line to Twitter is the same as Facebook and any other social media: Never say something bad about anything or anyone. I don't care how angry you are or how strong of an opinion you have, if you want to have control over your personal brand, keep your tweets sweet!

REMINDERS

Everything you write is an extension of who you are. Social media is nothing more than your virtual extension of yourself. Everything you write leaves a digital footprint, which is there forever—even if you delete it. Save yourself from embarrassment and all sorts of trouble. Control what you write and how you share. Stay away from everything and anything that someone else can use against you or allows others to see how you think, including your opinions and beliefs. In business, you will deal with people from all kinds of backgrounds, religions, political philosophies and social standings. Stay away from advertising where you stand on any given topic that can cause insult or controversy, and you will never have to worry about anything! Don't post pictures of yourself drinking shots of alcohol or dancing on a table top. If you do, keep them private. You are the only person who has complete control over your image; your personal brand. This is vital to your success in business. Protect it at all costs.

CHAPTER FOUR

Final Touches

As you continue to build upon and enhance your personal brand, know that the better and more respected your brand, the more successful you will be in business. Business is all about relationships and reputation. It doesn't really matter the school from which you graduated, your background or socio-economic level growing up. People will hire you and do business with you, if they like you and trust you. People skills have always rated as the top contributor to one's success. How you dress, speak and carry yourself is what will define how others perceive you. But, to truly refine yourself into a person whose brand is stellar, there are many other little details that will add to your brand and enhance your reputation and the way people respond to you.

This last chapter is about adding those finishing touches to yourself that will give you the edge in business and cause people to want to hire you and do business with you.

TOP TEN FINAL TOUCHES THAT WILL MAKE YOU A WINNER

1. COMPLIMENT, DON'T CRITICIZE

Everyone needs a compliment once in a while. Unfortunately, they are few and far in between. Instead, people are very fast to criticize. This is also one of the biggest problems with social media. People are more apt to say something negative than to say something kind or positive. Most are fast to point out what is wrong with someone or something than to recognize the good in someone or something. This is why you need to become one who compliments others and recognizes their achievements. If someone does something good, let them know. If someone demonstrates talent in a given area, recognize it. Failure to compliment and only to criticize is the hallmark of someone who is insecure. People will often overlook your shortcomings, if they like you and see you as someone who is kind, considerate and complimentary. Shower people with compliments and they will shower you with the same.

There may be occasions when a criticism is necessary. If someone is doing something incorrectly or made a mistake, you may need to point it out. But, there is a way to do this without making it a personal attack and causing the person to take offense. It is called constructive criticism. It involves critiquing the "thing," not the actual person, and should always involve recognition of the person's good qualities and reinforcement of their talents and abilities. For instance, if you are a manager and you realize that one of your employees made a mistake on a report, never point it out in front of others. Don't single them out and say that they are "irresponsible" or "sloppy" in their work. This will only cause them to resent you and will not bring out the best in them to do better. Try something like this: If your employee named Robert made a mistake on a report, ask to speak with him privately and say, *"Robert, first of all, I just wanted to tell you that I appreciate your hard work on this report. I know how time consuming and difficult it can be. I also know that another pair of eyes is always helpful. I was reading your report and I noticed that there was a mistake on some of the figures for March. I've done this myself in the past. But I wanted to draw your attention to it before we passed it on to upper management. Beside this, you did an outstanding job and I want to commend you."*

How does that compare with, *"Robert, what's the matter with you? Do you proofread your work? You made a mistake! You need to stop being so sloppy with your work."* In the first example, you are treating Robert like a human being and are respectful of him and his work. Mistakes are made by everyone. They are not necessarily a reflection of someone's intellect or inability. They are simply a mistake. By handling the situation as shown first, you complimented his work, recognized his abilities and raised him up, not tore him down. Robert will respect you for it and will do an even better job in the future because he will be motivated to do better.

Remember, offer compliments freely, but criticize constructively and never criticize the person, only the thing. Always use positive language and never leave someone feeling defeated or deflated. Doing so only diminishes you and demonstrates poor character, unprofessionalism and insecurity. Worse, others will not be motivated to do better in the future.

2. PLEASE AND THANK YOU

While we are all taught to say these two words as a child, sometimes we forget that we should use them abundantly and generously as adults. Please and thank you are the hallmarks of someone who is polite and refined. No matter the person, whether great or small, we should be in the habit of saying please and thank you to everyone. Don't just shower your boss, manager or supervisor with please and thank you, shower everyone with whom you come into contact who shows you the slightest courtesy. These should not be reserved for those whose favor you want to win. You want to be a better and bigger person than that. People will greatly appreciate it and will love and respect you for your polite nature. It shows that you appreciate everything people do—no matter who they are.

3. WRITE PERSONAL NOTES

In an age where everyone communicates through e-mail or texts, you will make an enormous impression on anyone when you take the time to handwrite a personal note to thank, compliment or congratulate them for something. A handwritten note is a rare item these days. It shows that you took the time to sit down and think about the words you will use without the benefit of spell check or a delete button. Someone helped you with something? Write them a note of thanks. Someone got a promotion? Send them a note of congratulations. A written note is very special and will be most appreciated. In fact, people keep written notes because they are so special. What's more, you will show yourself to be a very thoughtful person of great character and refinement. So, get yourself some personalized stationery and start writing notes to people. You will stand out from the rest if you do! It's also a good idea to keep track of clients', customers' or co-workers' birthdays to send them a birthday card.

4. OFFER A HELPING HAND

In business, we are never alone. We work with and encounter many people in various positions. Selfishness will ultimately leave us all alone. Instead, seek opportunities to offer a helpful hand to a fellow employee with something on which he or she may be working. If the custodian is carrying in supplies, hold the door and perhaps offer to help carry some items. If someone in the office needs assistance with a project, the creation of a PowerPoint or maybe advice on how to help a customer or client, always be the first to offer a helping hand. Not only will this prove your kindness, but others will always be there to assist you.

5.   STAND WHEN APPROACHED

If you are seated and anyone—whether it is a boss, secretary or client—walks up to you to shake your hand, immediately stand up and greet them. While the Pope is expected to remain seated when he is greeted, we are not the Pope. Standing up shows respect and puts you both on a level playing field. It is the proper thing to do; failing to do it shows immaturity, or worse, arrogance. You most certainly never want to come across as either. Show people how refined and polished you are and always stand when approached. It is also important to remain standing until a person of higher rank, such as your boss, a client or your interviewer is first seated.

6.   MIND YOUR OWN BUSINESS

This is one of the hardest things for people to learn. Unfortunately, humans are addicted to drama. They cannot resist gossip. They inevitably repeat things they hear and talk about other people when they are not around. The office or your place of work is no exception. If you really want to distinguish yourself and have a stellar reputation, learn how to mind your own business. A truly successful person never lowers her or himself to gossip. It is the mark of those who have little to do and too much time on their hands. If you want to be successful, you should be too busy to engage in gossip. You also should never engage in it because it only diminishes you and winds up hurting others and causing personal pain. Gossip around an office is a prescription for lower employee morale and less productivity.

Let's face it, you wouldn't like it if someone were to gossip about you, would you? No, you wouldn't. Gossip is a terrible thing and one of the worst aspects of human behavior. Unless you are saying something kind or offering a compliment, walk away from gossip. If you never repeat things told to you in confidence, never read something not intended for your eyes, and never listen in on a conversation not intended for your ears, how could anyone ever get mad at you? In business, the trust and reputation you build and establish is what will make people like you. People do business with those they like. And they like those they can trust. Rise above the drama and nonsense of gossip and always mind your own business within the confines of your work and business relationships.

7. AVOID COARSE LANGUAGE

The F-bomb is alive and well in the vocabulary of many people. Off-color jokes, sexual remarks and other vulgarities are unfortunately a part of our modern daily dialogue. But a true professional never uses coarse language in public or in a mixed setting. The use of coarse language does not serve to make you unique. It will not make you seem extraordinary. It will only make you seem ordinary. If you do use coarse language, keep it in your private domain. Keep it to your inner circle of friends and in your home. Don't allow it to enter into your vocabulary in business. Its use in public denotes a lack of vocabulary, intelligence and refinement. Avoid writing it or even using abbreviations on social media, such as "wtf?" It is totally classless. If you write it, it is the same as if you were saying it.

Don't lower yourself in the eyes of others. Hold yourself to a higher standard and keep your words clean when you deal with clients, customers or business associates.

8. NEVER PRESUME UPON A FRIENDSHIP

Don't become someone who is always imposing upon others. Don't develop a reputation in the workplace or among your business associates as one who is always asking for favors. The rule to follow as a professional is never to ask someone to do something you would not be willing to do for them. Asking someone for a favor is fine. But be sure to extend yourself to that person, as well. Ask kindly and always offer your appreciation of their kindness. When someone in your place of business does something for you, thank them and remind them that you appreciate their help and that you are there to assist them at any time. If you don't, you'll develop a reputation as a "user" or a "taker". Be a giver, instead. Be ready, willing and able to help anyone. Shower them with appreciation and, even better, as I said above, write them a thank you note.

9. BE KIND

Who doesn't like a kind person? Kindness brings out the very best in everyone. It is the way we demonstrate humanity at its best. It is the "human thing to do." Be kind to everyone in your life and career. Allow it to shine forth from your soul. Let it exude from every pore. We all wish we lived in a world where everyone was kind. Well, making that a reality begins with your own displays of kindness. Kindness involves treating others as you would want to be treated. Saying hello, smiling, offering assistance, support and putting others ahead of you are all acts of kindness that should be exhibited by everyone. Success in your career will be a certainty when you develop a reputation for being kind as part of your personal brand. No harm can come from it. It will cause you to be the recipient of everyone's esteem.

10. SHOW HUMILITY

Finally, the greatest trait any person can possess is humility. Humility is what makes all of the above traits so easy to display. Humility is the flower of humanity. If you think highly of yourself, feel you are more important than others and always seek to be in front, you will only wind up losing in the end. A person of humility puts others before or ahead of her or his self. Because of this, the true person of humility is raised up by everyone around her or him. It is a simple little rule for life and, once understood and practiced, will earn more honor, acclaim and attention for you than any pretense or false front you could ever try to display. I am amazed at how many people falsely believe that to get ahead in their career they need to walk over everyone else. Forget what you see in the movies. In real life, those who treat others with respect and seek to avoid their own headlines wind up getting more attention and find far more success in their career than any false ego could ever think to achieve. Humility is the secret to building your personal brand. It evokes the goodness and kindness from others and is the key to being a refined and respected professional.

Conclusion

You may be asking yourself, "With all of the years I've spent in school and all of the money spent on my education, if these skills are so very basic and are what increase the likelihood of my success, why was I not taught them?" That's a very good question. The long answer is that these skills have traditionally been more societal. It was assumed you learned them at home, from the family, within and among your social circles and in relationships. They were displayed in the media, the movies and television shows, as well as, among our leaders, clergy and politicians. They represented a standard to which everyone in society adhered—regardless of their age, background, race, religion, culture or socio-economic background.

People skills and character are not the property of any single group. Their affect is universal among all people because everyone would rather be with someone they like. People would prefer to do business with someone on whom they can rely and, most important, everyone wants to be respected.

The short answer is that we've lost the universal framework within our society. We've forgotten the basic standards which are quite simple. We've changed our view from each being a contributing member of a greater, overall society to one where society is here to serve the individual. We expect that respect is automatic, not earned. We demand others to accept us, but fail to accept others. We've changed our point-of-view from "What's best for everyone?" to "What's best for me?" The dirty little secret, though, is that by failing to observe this greater role, we have actually robbed ourselves of a greater individual career.

This, however, should by no means be mistaken as a call to lose our individuality; quite the contrary. This is a call for a greater individuality; one whose substance only adds to how we are seen and perceived and—most of all—respected by others in our lives and careers. We wonder, sometimes, how we, as one small person in this big world can make a difference. The truth is that only as individuals—only when we each choose to be the best that we can be—to put our best face forward in all that we do—can we each become the greatest we can. And in business, that is the recipe for success.

Aside from broadening your view of yourself in the world of business and how your character and people skills can bring you success, if there is a synopsis of this book which you can take away, it would be this:

Choose to learn how to act successfully, speak successfully and dress successfully. But above all, combine those with solid character, respect and kindness. That is all that is needed to make your idea of a successful career become your reality.

There is one little extra bit of advice that you should follow. Whatever you choose or have chosen to do for your career, be sure to choose something you love, something that will make you happy and to which you can look forward each and every day to arise from bed and set out to do. The word "work" is a four letter word. It has a negative connotation. Doing what you love and that which gives you a sense of fulfillment will never seem like "work." It will become your lifestyle and one that will give you great joy. This joy will exude from inside of you and will affect everyone around you. And, if you are already on your career path, use this as a means to reinvigorate yourself and become the successful businessperson you can be.

Learn to embody the skills in this book. See yourself as the spoke on the larger wheel of life. Life can be as wondrous as you make it. So when you set out on a course in your career, let it become your life and allow your greatness to add to the greater whole of humanity.

I wish you the greatest success and a life wrought with peace—for you and for all humankind.

About the Author

Brian Haggerty has the rare ability to teach, inform, and influence people while simultaneously making them laugh and boosting their self-confidence. His smooth, but powerful voice captures the attention of audiences immediately, while his dynamic and thought-provoking performances create lasting impressions, and make Brian one of the most successful educational public speakers.

Since 2005, Brian has served his local New Jersey community in the role of Commissioner of Public Works, and as Head of the Department of Public Affairs. Through consistent goodwill, honesty, and humor, Brian has proved himself a unique and positive force in his community, capable of engaging minds, and inspiring hearts—especially young ones.

During his many years in politics, Brian's countless public speeches have led the charge toward positive change, and irrefutably improved the lives of people in his community. Brian believes, however, that any natural talents for public speaking were passed down through his family. From an early age, he loved to hear stories of his grandfather, a New Jersey attorney whose courtroom manner was so dazzling that people would take the bus to the Hackensack Court House just to witness him try a case. His father (who also worked tirelessly in government) was also a tremendous public speaker, while his mother (a school teacher of four decades) perfected his grammar, and fine-tuned his manners.

Brian Haggerty's mass appeal as an educational speaker came after his three-part series entitled, "Mannerly Speaking." After decades of receiving compliments on his voice, Brian finally combined his speaking, teaching, and entertaining skills to present a subject about which he was passionate. Following the event, business leaders, school officials, and community advocates lost no time in contacting Brian in the hope that he might share his popular 'info-tainment' speaking style with other audiences.

The key to Brian's great success, not only as a public speaker, but as a politician, and a businessman, lies in his unique ability to:

- Inspire and motivate people to be the best they can be.

- Empower each and every individual, from all areas, backgrounds, and ages, with the gift of who they are and how they can do anything they wish.

- Illuminate before audiences the great value of civility and the importance of how we present ourselves publicly.

- Demonstrate with kindness, how each one of us has a responsibility to conduct his or herself with graciousness, compassion, strong character, and a respect for all people.

A generous and engaging raconteur, Brian shares stories, anecdotes and personal experiences from his life to demonstrate how each principle he teaches has shaped and formed his approach to these ideals. While his personality and delivery is similar for all audiences, stories and experiences are chosen to perfectly fit the audience being addressed.

When speaking to students, Brian harkens back to his own thoughts and feelings when he was in school as a teenager. On a corporate level, Brian shares his political, business and social experiences to explore the same principles, but from a perspective more fitting for the executive.

> *"Over the years, building trust and relationships was the key to our success in business and politics. And in order to have successful relationships, I had to embody every ounce of good character, responsibility and being of my word."*
>
> —*Brian Haggerty*

Brian believes that effective business leaders can learn to refine themselves, expand their knowledge of social and business etiquette, improve upon their communication skills, develop charisma, presence, and strengthen self-confidence for any social or business setting.

> *"When we each adhere to a solid, universal framework for our behavior, our manners and the graciousness and civility we demonstrate to all, not only increase our level of personal success but make the world a better place for everyone to succeed."*
>
> —*Brian Haggerty*

Brian is heavily in demand when it comes to addressing young people. He believes that students can learn the importance of good character and how they can achieve success through solid social and business relationships. He understands that young people can learn how to carry and conduct themselves, learn how to speak well and communicate effectively, and learn how to make the greatest impression upon everyone they meet as they surge into the world as empowered young individuals.

Brian Haggerty feels the greatest sense of joy and accomplishment from using his gift as a public speaker to move, motivate, and inspire his audiences. He is not only a revered public figure, with years of experience in business and government, but also a man who believes in the potential we all have to be great and to be generous—not only at work or in school, but in every task we set our minds to.

Brian Haggerty has a gift for reuniting people with the beauty and the power of their own lives, and for providing them with the tools to become the people they always dreamed they could be. He delivers quality information with such fun, generosity, and charisma, that audiences can't help but chant his name.

You may find out more about the author at http://www.brianhaggertyspeaks.com/ and friend him on Facebook or follow him on Twitter at @BHSpeaks.

Made in the USA
Charleston, SC
30 January 2014